IRELAND

CHARMING SMALL HOTEL GUIDES

IRELAND

EDITED BY

Jenny Rees

DUNCAN PETERSEN

HUNTER
PUBLISHING

Conceived, designed and produced by
Duncan Petersen Publishing Ltd

Editorial Director Andrew Duncan
Contributing Editor Nicola Swallow
Production Editor Nicola Davies
Art Director Mel Petersen
Designers Christopher Foley
Beverley Stewart
Maps Christopher Foley

This edition published 2000 by
Duncan Petersen Publishing Ltd,
31 Ceylon Road, London W14 OPY

Sales representation and distribution in the U.K. and Ireland by
Portfolio Books Limited
Unit 1C, West Ealing Business Centre
Alexandria Road
London W13 0NJ
Tel: 0181 579 7748

ISBN 1 872576 95 8

A CIP catalogue record for this book is available
from the British Library

AND

Published in the USA by
Hunter Publishing Inc.,
130 Campus Drive, Edison, N.J. 08818.
Tel (732) 225 1900 Fax (732) 417 0482
For details on hundreds of other travel guides and language courses, visit
Hunter's Web site at hunterpublishing.com

ISBN 1-55650-892-1

Typeset by Duncan Petersen Publishing Ltd
Printed by G. Canale & Co SpA, Turin

CONTENTS

INTRODUCTION

THIS IS THE SIXTEENTH TITLE in Duncan Petersen's now
well-established *Charming Small Hotel Guides*. Some
of our readers may wonder why it has taken us so long to
include Ireland in the series. We were, naturally, waiting
for signs of a lasting solution to the cross-border troubles
which have kept many tourists away. But recently visitors
have begun to return to Ulster, to the marvellous scenery of
the North Antrim coast, the Mountains of Mourne and the
lakes of Co Fermanagh, and we can but hope that the
publication of this book really will coincide with the start
of a positive new chapter in the island's long, eventful and
often turbulent history. We have always included a small
section on Ireland in editions of *Charming Small Hotel
Guides* to Britain, but in this new all-Ireland title we are
able to give the full picture of Ireland's charming places to
stay, comprising, of course, not only hotels, but castles,
great houses, country houses, converted cottages and
stables, farmhouses, town houses and restaurants with
rooms, all within a wide range of prices and all with our
special qualities of character and charm.

IN THIS INTRODUCTORY SECTION

Ireland for the traveller

In a sense, what could be more perfect for the traveller than a small and beautiful island with a temperate climate, and famously leisurely way of life? The Emerald Isle has more than its fair share of gifts. Roughly about 150 miles across and a little more than 250 miles from north to south, it is a country of contrasts and changing light, of mountains, lakes and rivers, lush green pastures, bog and wild moorland, and 2,000 miles of coastline with small rocky coves, long sandy beaches, and some of the highest cliffs in Europe. In some of the more remote parts of the country you can drive for miles without seeing anything else but sheep. But if you want bright lights, music and good food, Ireland has excellent chefs to cook the abundant produce of their native land and pubs galore that nightly celebrate the traditional Irish love of music and conversation.

It is not a place to hurry through, or you will miss too much on the way. Looking at the map can be deceptive. Getting from A to B may look easy, but the journey will usually take much longer than you expected, particularly when visiting all those long fingers of land penetrating into the sea in the South-West. Ireland can be very busy in the summer during the holiday season, and there can even be traffic jams in places that are quite empty for the rest of the year. If you can manage it, the spring or autumn months are the time to be there. And believe what they say about Ireland - that it wouldn't be so green and beautiful if it didn't rain so much. It does rain, and it rains a great deal. We were pleased to see that an increasing number of hotels and country houses are realizing how much guests appreciate a swimming pool, sauna or steam room for those rainy, misty days when it is not possible to go out, and we have noted these assets wherever we found them.

Our criteria

Our selection criteria are the same in Ireland as they are anywhere. We aim to include only those places that are in some way captivating, with a distinctive personality, and which offer a truly personal service. While being highly selective, we also give as broad a range of recommendations as possible, to suit all budgets; and as hotels are often fully booked, it is useful to have alternatives.

In Ireland, as elswhere in Europe, we found many hotels which easily satisfied our highly selective approach, but there are a significant number which, though basically recommendable, for one reason or another fall short of our ideal. The description of each hotel makes this distinction clear. However, be assured that all the hotels in the guide are, one way or another, true to the concept of the charming small hotel. If you find any more, please let us know (see page 32).

In making our selection, we have been careful to bear in mind the many different requirements of our readers. Some will be backpackers; others will be millionaires; the vast majority will fall between the two.

Charming and small

Ideally, our recommendations have fewer than 30 bedrooms, but this is not a rigid requirement. Many hotels with more than 30 bedrooms feel much smaller, and you will find such places in this guide. We attach more importance to size than other guides because we think that unless a hotel is small, it cannot give a genuinely personal welcome, or make you feel like an individual, rather than just a guest. Unlike other guides, we often rule out places that have great qualities, but are nevertheless no more nor less than – hotels. Our hotels are special in some way.

We think that we have a much clearer idea than other guides of what is special and what is not: and we think we apply these criteria more consistently than other guides because we are a small and personally managed company rather than a bureaucracy. We have a small team of like-minded inspectors, thoroughly rehearsed in recognizing what we want. While we very much appreciate readers' reports – see below – they are not our main source of information.

Whole-page entries

We rarely see all these qualities together in one place; but our warmest recommendations – whole-page, with photograph – usually lack only one or two of these qualities.

Half-page entries

Don't, however, ignore our half-page entries. They are very useful addresses, and all are charming small hotels. You can't have stars on every page.

No fear or favour

Unlike many guides, there is no payment for inclusion. The selection is made entirely independently.

Choosing your room

Many of our selections have rooms which are similar in both price and quality, but others, while remaining the same in price, are much more varied in quality. Where possible, we have given as much detail as we can about rooms and their position in the house or hotel; where there are balconies or ground floor rooms opening on to the garden or courtyard, these have been mentioned. We have also referred to annexes where they exist. Annexes, being new additions, can often be more comfortable and better-equipped than older bedrooms and bathrooms, so don't discount them.

Range of accommodation

In the past, the small hotel has earned itself a doubtful name in Ireland. The term usually meant some not-very-comfortable or attractive rooms above a noisy bar. But in the past ten years or so, the Irish hospitality business has undergone great change and small hotels of character have been emerging. Tourism has

SO WHAT EXACTLY DO WE LOOK FOR?

- *A peaceful, attractive setting in an interesting and picturesque position.*

- *A building that is either handsome or interesting or historic, or at least with a distinct character.*

- *Bedrooms that are well proportioned with as much character as the public rooms below.*

- *Ideally, we look for adequate space, but on a human scale: we don't go for places that rely on grandeur, or that have pretensions that could intimidate.*

- *Decorations must be harmonious and in good taste, and the furnishings and facilities comfortable and well maintained. We like to see interesting antique furniture that is there because it can be used, not simply revered.*

- *The proprietors and staff need to be dedicated and thoughtful, offering a personal welcome, without being intrusive. The guest needs to feel like an individual.*

brought increasing prosperity to many parts of Ireland and travel, not only for tourists, but for innkeepers, hoteliers and hosts in general, has opened all kinds of new horizons. Ireland has a wide range of accommodation such as farmhouses, townhouses, suburban houses, guest houses, country houses, heritage houses, family-run and smaller commercially-owned hotels. Some of the guest houses we have chosen are by no means small. They are often large and Georgian and standing in acres of parkland. The country house is very much part of Ireland's history and now plays an important role in attracting visitors: there seems to be no end to the fascination for the 'upstairs-downstairs' life that was once routine for these big country houses, as the huge membership of the National Trust shows. These houses used to be busy places, small communities in themselves; to see them empty and abandoned is sad, and it is heartening to see their rooms and gardens filled with people again.

Bathrooms
In the big houses, some dressing-rooms, of a reasonable size, have been successfully adapted to make bathrooms. But in many country houses – and in Georgian Dublin - it has not been possible to provide generous-sized bathrooms adjoining bedrooms, without

taking out walls, putting in partitions, cutting out corners of original plasterwork and altering the shape and symmetry of rooms. Sometimes the bathroom is across the corridor and possibly shared with other rooms. In this case you may be supplied with a dressing gown. So if you want a bathroom 'en suite' with your bedroom, check at the time of booking. In Ireland, the term 'bathroom' does not always mean that there is a bath tub: there could be just a shower. Once again, check when booking. To many people, being able to rely on a long, hot soak in the bathtub at the end of a day's walking, fishing, or cycling can make all the difference to a holiday.

'En suite' is one of the weasel words of the guest business.It is not used in France, where one might expect it to have come from. You will not find it used in our entries, although on many occasions we were told that bedrooms were 'en suite', whereas what was really the case was that bedrooms had adjoining shower rooms.

The long table

Many country houses seat guests around a long table for dinner – and for breakfast, too. Sometimes this works, and sometimes it does not. Some people fail to understand other people's jokes. Some, such as couples who have gone away for a romantic few days together, wish, like Greta Garbo, to be alone. Interestingly, the long table seems to cause people fewest problems at breakfast; at dinner, differences seem to surface more readily. In fact, we have found that quite a few hosts have now had enough of communal dining, and in many dining-rooms you will find a selection of tables, as in a restaurant, that can be used in different ways. So that, for example, two couples who got on at breakfast are put together for dinner.

Tourist information

Addresses and contact numbers for tourist information offices for each section are listed with the relevant maps on pages 19 - 31. Most large towns - and some of the larger villages - have tourist offices offering information on local events, museums, craft shops, attractions and festivals. In Ireland, tourist office staff are very helpful and the offices have a large and comprehensive collection of brochures and written material.

Getting there

Major airports in the Republic of Ireland are Dublin, Shannon, Cork and Knock (in the west); smaller ones are Kerry International, between Tralee and Killarney, Galway, Sligo, Carrickfinn (Co Donegal) and Waterford. Two airports serve Belfast: Belfast International Airport at Aldergrove, 15 miles (24 km) from the city, handles all international traffic; Belfast City Airport, 4 miles (6 km) from the city, handles local and UK flights only. Car hire is available at all airports.

Pet likes

These are some of the things that we have particularly appreciated and noted in many of the hotels in which we have stayed. Maybe they will strike you, too.

- Wonderful old buildings, sympathetically restored.
- Hotels in superb positions with glorious views.
- Spotlessly clean bedrooms and bathrooms.
- Good quality linen and comfortable pillows.
- Beautiful gardens, with seats arranged so that you can sit out.
- Large beds with good mattresses.
- Fresh flowers.
- Bathtubs and plenty of instant hot water.
- Freshly baked bread for breakfast.

Pet hates

- Too many bathrooms with shower only.
- Serve-yourself sideboard breakfasts that look as if they may be recycled.
- Staff in airline-type uniform.
- Reception desks with staff that are either absent or too busy to help.
- Guests' cars parked outside windows so that they spoil wonderful views.
- No reading light by the bed.
- Excessive use of sweetly-scented air freshener.

How to find an entry

In this guide, the whole-page entries, beginning on page 33, come first, followed by the half-page entries, which begin on page 119.

We have divided Ireland into six sections: North (includes Ulster); West; South-West; South-East; Dublin; Central. Within

---

FOR VISITORS FROM OUTSIDE EUROPE

First-time visitors to European countries, especially when they get to rural areas, are often surprised by the following:

- Facecloths and Kleenex tissues are not always provided as standard items.

- Private bathrooms with rooms aren't necessarily a standard feature.

- Floor numbers. What Americans call the first floor is known in Britain as the ground floor or '0'.

- Elevators are known as lifts in Ireland.

- Parking lot is a term you won't encounter. You'll see 'Parking' or just a 'P' sign.

these sections the entries are arranged in alphabetical order by nearest town. If several occur in one town, they are arranged in alphabetical order by name of hotel. The half-page entries follow the same pattern.

To find a hotel in a particular area, use the maps following this introduction to locate the appropriate pages.

To locate a specific hotel, whose name you know, or a hotel in a place you know, use the indexes at the back, which list entries both by name and by nearest place name.

How to read an entry

At the top of each entry is a coloured bar highlighting the place, followed by a categorisation which gives some clue to its character. These categories are, as far as possible, self-explanatory.

Fact boxes

The fact box given for each hotel follows a standard pattern: the explanation that follows is for full- and half-page entries.

Tel and Fax The first part of the number given in our entries is the area code within Ireland.

If you are calling a number inside the Irish Republic from abroad, drop the initial zero of the area code, after dialling the international code, which is 00353; for Northern Ireland it is 00 44. However, to call Northern Ireland from Britain, you don't need the international code.

As we went to press, telephone numbers in both the Republic of Ireland and Northern Ireland were being changed. Where we were aware of a new telephone number we have listed it. In April 2000, the area code for Northern Ireland became 028; all local five- and six-digit numbers became eight digits.

E-mail This is becoming more and more popular; a quick and efficient way to book for both parties. One country hotel we visited in Co Cork was taking 80 per cent of bookings by e-mail.

Websites are listed when available.

Location The location and setting of the hotel are briefly described and any useful information included to help you find your way there. Where parking is provided or available, we have made a note.

Meals Under this heading we list the meals available on the premises.

We do not state whether a hotel provides room service, as this can vary. If in doubt, check in advance with the selected hotel.

Prices Prices in the Republic of Ireland are given in Irish punt – referred to in this guide as I£. Its value is roughly the same as that of the £ sterling, but it is tied to the Euro and so fluctuates. Northern Ireland's currency is the £ sterling.

Very few hotels we visited for this guide have one price for a room, but there are exceptions. We have quoted the price per person in a shared room in high season, and then given the overall price of a standard double. Most hotels have a higher price for single residency of a room. If your visit is out of season, then you are likely to be given a pleasant surprise, as the price will be lower than the one we have quoted. If breakfast is included in the price (which it generally is) we say so; otherwise we give the price of breakfast separately. They believe in big breakfasts in Ireland. In the south, the full Irish fry consists of bacon, eggs, sausage, black/white pudding, soda bread; in Northern Ireland, the Ulster fry may not have black/white pudding, but potato cake. After eating the full breakfast, most people need only a light lunch.

Where we have given lunch prices, these are mainly the price of a light or bar lunch, such as soup and a sandwich. Where we give dinner prices, this is normally the price of the table d'hôte, which will change daily.

Unless half-board is obligatory in a hotel, we have not mentioned its cost. But it is always worth asking in advance, because there are some very good deals to be had, especially over two- and three-day stays.

Above all, check the price first. Sometimes prices go up after we have gone to press. Sometimes there is a seasonal or other variation from the printed version.

Rooms Under this heading we indicate the number and type of room – and whether the rooms have baths (usually with shower or shower attachment as well) or just showers.

Facilities Under facilities we list: public rooms, lift, courtyard; garden, terrace or sitting-out area; outdoor or indoor swimming pool; tennis court; sauna, steam room, and fitness facilities.

Credit cards We use the following abbreviations:

AE	American Express
DC	Diners Club
MC	MasterCard (Access)
V	Visa (Barclaycard/Bank Americard)

Children Children are often welcome, but not always, and where this is so we have made note. We have made a distinction between children being 'welcome' and children being 'accepted'. Many private houses with precious antiques and furnishings would rather not accept children; others have guests who have come for peace and quiet. Some hotels and households do not like children in the dining-room in the evenings, and provide high tea at 6pm.

Disabled Many of our entries welcome disabled guests although they do not have special facilities; many have special facilities. We have noted where there are ground floor bedrooms or a lift.

Pets Almost everywhere you go in the country in Ireland you will see fields bursting with livestock: sheep; cattle; horses. In many places you will see very expensive horses. So be careful: dogs should be kept on a lead if there is the slightest risk of a problem. When it comes to dogs in hotels, you will find a wide variety of house rules, ranging from absolutely no dogs permitted anywhere on the premises to small dogs being allowed to sleep in their baskets in bedrooms. Hosts have to think of other guests – they don't want complaints. They don't want dogs scratching at paintwork on bedroom doors trying to get out, or anxiously whining while waiting for their owners to return. However, it is widely accepted that one of the reasons why Ireland is popular with travellers from the British mainland is because there is no quarantine required and British dogs may go on holiday with their owners. Generally, few objections will be made to your dog spending the night in the car. Most hosts will do their best to accommodate if they can. Many hotels and houses have kennels. Even if your dog is not permitted in the bedroom, you may be given a room near the staircase down to the front door so that you can make regular trips to see your pet in the car during the night and be near in case you hear barking.

If you wish to travel with your dog in Ireland, it's best not to leave anything to chance. Travel with a basket and bedding; bottled water in hot weather; bowls for water and food.

Closed There is quite a variety of closing times and the dates we have given are those supplied to us by the hotel or guest house.

The final entry in the fact box is the name of the **Proprietor(s)**. Where the hotel is run by a manager, we give his or her name.

THE HIDDEN IRELAND

Where you see a reference to Hidden Ireland houses in the guide, this refers to the group of Irish country houses that welcome guests looking for something a little different. These are not hotels, guest houses or bed-and-breakfasts, but buildings of architectural merit and great character; they all play and have played a part in Ireland's social – and sometimes political – history. Some have belonged to the same family for centuries and the present owners – your hosts – all enjoy sharing their homes with appreciative visitors. Many of these houses have not changed much over the years. So, don't expect a reception desk, bar or residents' sitting-room. Expect instead a warm welcome and a glass of sherry beside a log fire in a comfortable drawing-room filled with family heirlooms.

Some are great houses, at the centre of large estates. They may have been designed by well-known architects and lived in or visited by distinguished people. Others are smaller, but no less beautiful or interesting. Most are surrounded by their own tree-studded parks or by gardens, often internationally renowned.

Hidden Ireland suggests that just one night may not give you nearly enough time to see the house and its surroundings properly – or to get to know your hosts. They strongly urge staying for two or three nights in order to relax fully and to absorb the atmosphere and settle in to the daily life of the house.

Staying in one of these places you will probably be a member of a house party – albeit one where there is a bill at the end of the stay. It is usual for the guests to change for dinner, though not into anything very formal, as a courtesy to the other guests and to the host and hostess – indeed, to the house itself.

You may well see rather little of the hostess in the evening, as she will be working in the kitchen. It is also possible that you may feel a little uncomfortable witnessing someone who owns a house as big as a palace occupying him – or herself with housekeeping and cooking. Don't give it a second thought: they are doing it because they get satisfaction from it – or at least, they should be. They want you to enjoy your stay.

And remember, as a paying guest, you are making a useful contribution to the maintenance of the house. No service charge is made on the bill, but if you wish to leave a tip for any staff, this is at your discretion and will be appreciated.

Some of these private houses are not suitable for children. Many have lakes and rivers; others may have precious antiques and furnishings. Check before booking.

A majority of bedrooms in these places will have their own private adjoining bathroom, but sometimes your bathroom may be across the corridor, and sometimes it may be shared. Again, check before booking.

An illustrated pocket-sized directory of heritage houses with guest accommodation (price I£3) is available from:

> *The Hidden Ireland*,
> 37 Lower Baggot Street,
> DUBLIN 2,
> IRELAND.
> Tel: +353 1 662 7166
> Fax: +353 1 662 7144
> Toll free in USA: 1800 688 0299
> E-mail: reservations@hidden-ireland.com

USEFUL ADDRESSES

Irish Tourist Board offices (Bord Fáilte):

Ireland
Baggot Street Bridge,
DUBLIN 2
Tel: 01 602 4000
Fax: 01 602 4100

London
150 New Bond Street,
LONDON W1Y 0AQ
Tel: 0207 518 0800
Fax: 0207 493 9065
E-mail: info@irishtouristboard.co.uk

New York
345 Park Avenue,
NEW YORK, NY10154
Tel: 212 418 0800
Fax: 212 371 9052

Northern Ireland Tourist Board offices:
E-mail: info@nitb.com

London
24 Haymarket,
LONDON SW1Y 4DG
Tel: 0541 555 250
Fax: 0171 766 9929

Belfast
59 North Street,
BELFAST BT1 1NB
Northern Ireland
Tel: 01232 246609
Fax: 01232 240960

New York
551 Fifth Avenue, Suite 701,
NEW YORK, NY10176
Tel: 212 922 0101 or 800-326-0036
Fax: 212 922 0099

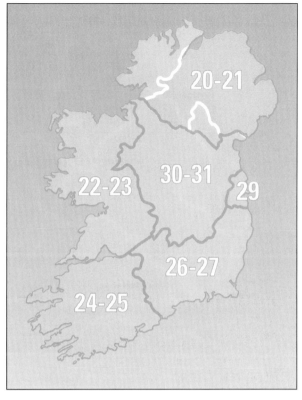

HOTEL LOCATION MAPS

North 20-21

West 22-23

South-West 24-25

South-East 26-27

Dublin 28-29

Central 30-31

NORTH

Ulster's six counties have some of the most spectacular and beautiful landscapes in Ireland, from the famous Giant's Causeway and the Antrim
coast – where on a fine day you can see the Scottish lowlands – to the
Mountains of Mourne 'that sweep down to the sea', the Glens of Antrim
and the lakes of Co Fermanagh. Armagh, the ecclesiastical capital, walled
Londonderry, and Belfast, the Victorian boom town, are the three historic
cities of a country that is about the size of Yorkshire or Connecticut. To
the west are the mountains of Co Donegal, where the rugged coastline is
battered by the Atlantic. All the colours of Donegal tweed can be found in
sheep-strewn hillsides and moorland, bogs, loughs and the wilderness of
Glenveagh National Park.

Tourist Information Offices

59 North Street,
BELFAST, NI
Tel: 028 9024 6609

40 English Street,
ARMAGH, NI
Tel: 028 37521800

44 Foyle Street,
LONDONDERRY, NI
Tel: 028 7126 7284

Wellington Road,
ENNISKILLEN, NI
Tel: 028 6632 3110

Derry Road,
LETTERKENNY,
Co Donegal
Tel: 074 21160

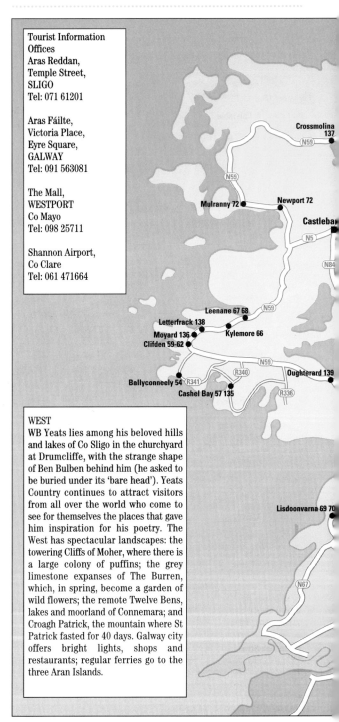

Tourist Information
Offices
Aras Reddan,
Temple Street,
SLIGO
Tel: 071 61201

Aras Fáilte,
Victoria Place,
Eyre Square,
GALWAY
Tel: 091 563081

The Mall,
WESTPORT
Co Mayo
Tel: 098 25711

Shannon Airport,
Co Clare
Tel: 061 471664

Crossmolina 137

N59

N59

Mulranny 72

Newport 72

Castlebar

N5

N84

Leenane 67 68　N59

Letterfrack 138

Moyard 136　　Kylemore 66

Clifden 59-62

N59

Oughterard 139

Ballyconneely 54　R341　　　R340

R336

Cashel Bay 57 135

Lisdoonvarna 69 70

N67

WEST

WB Yeats lies among his beloved hills and lakes of Co Sligo in the churchyard at Drumcliffe, with the strange shape of Ben Bulben behind him (he asked to be buried under its 'bare head'). Yeats Country continues to attract visitors from all over the world who come to see for themselves the places that gave him inspiration for his poetry. The West has spectacular landscapes: the towering Cliffs of Moher, where there is a large colony of puffins; the grey limestone expanses of The Burren, which, in spring, become a garden of wild flowers; the remote Twelve Bens, lakes and moorland of Connemara; and Croagh Patrick, the mountain where St Patrick fasted for 40 days. Galway city offers bright lights, shops and restaurants; regular ferries go to the three Aran Islands.

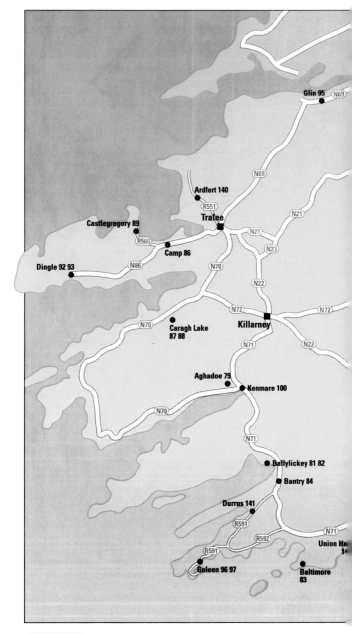

SOUTH-WEST

The spectacular natural beauty and changing light of the region is bewitching. Along the relatively unspoilt West Cork coast, long fingers of land stretch out into the sea and trawlers return to little fishing villages with their catch of fresh seafood. Kinsale, with its numerous restaurants, is said to be the 'gourmet' capital of Ireland, while the area has produced an abundance of talented chefs, many of them cooking in the kitchens of

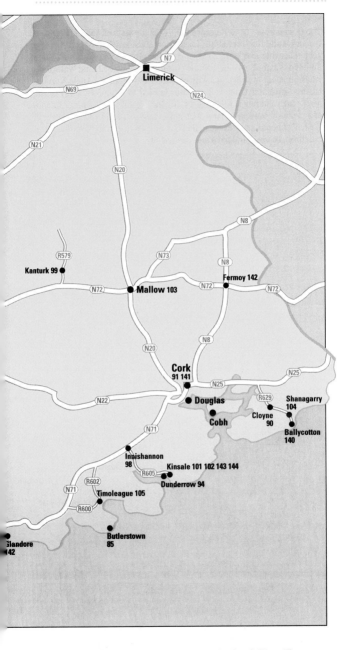

the top country house hotels spread across the South-West. The green 'Kingdom' of Kerry has its own rich treasures: a gorgeous coastline with clear blue waters warmed by the Gulf Stream and sunsets to be remembered forever; the haunting and romantic landscape of the Lakes of Killarney and surrounding mountains. The pace of life is slow, there's time to savour the good things in life. But the area gets crowded in summer.

SOUTH-EAST

The ferries come in to Rosslare and for many visitors the first sight of Ireland is the rich farmlands, leafy woodlands, fertile river valleys, and golden beaches and rocky coves of this much-invaded region. The Vikings founded Wexford, now best known for its opera festival, and Waterford, whose name is synonymous with crystal. Then came the Anglo-Norman barons, and later Cromwell's armies landed to desecrate many of the area's early churches. Kilkenny, briefly the capital, is the finest example of a medieval town in Ireland, with a Norman castle and 13thC cathedral; Cashel's famous and dramatic Rock, with its remarkable grey cluster of buildings, is one of Ireland's most visited sites.

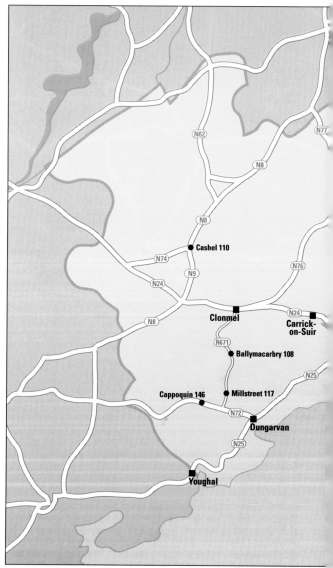

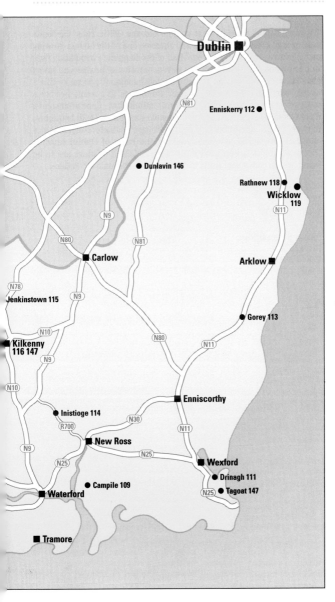

Tourist Information Offices

41 The Quay,
WATERFORD
Tel: 051 875823

Shee Alms House,
Rose Inn Street,
KILKENNY
Tel: 056 51500

Crescent Quay,
WEXFORD
Tel: 053 23111

Rialto House,
Fitzwilliam Square,
WICKLOW
Tel: 0404 69117

DUBLIN

The economic success of what is known as the Celtic Tiger has made Dublin, city of Georgian streets and squares, one of the fastest-growing urban centres in Western Europe. Half of the Republic's population lives in Dublin and her suburbs, and a new generation of prosperous young professionals mixes with the large student community to make this a young, swinging place; not surprisingly, Dublin has, as a result, become a top tourist destination. The shiny, minimalist Conran-designed Fitzwilliam Hotel and cobblestoned Temple Bar quarter, with boutiques, picture galleries, restaurants and cafés, are indicators of the city's changing times and new fortunes. But the heart of Dublin remains Georgian, and it is here that most of our selected lodgings are to be found, within convenient walking distance of all the main attractions.

Suffolk Street,
DUBLIN 2
Tel: 01 605 7799

Baggot Street Bridge,
DUBLIN 2
Tel: 01 602 4000

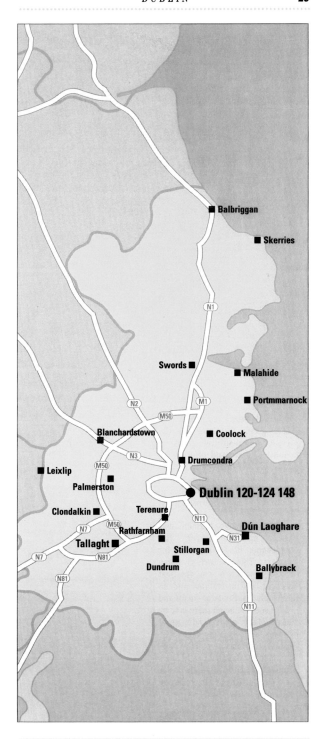

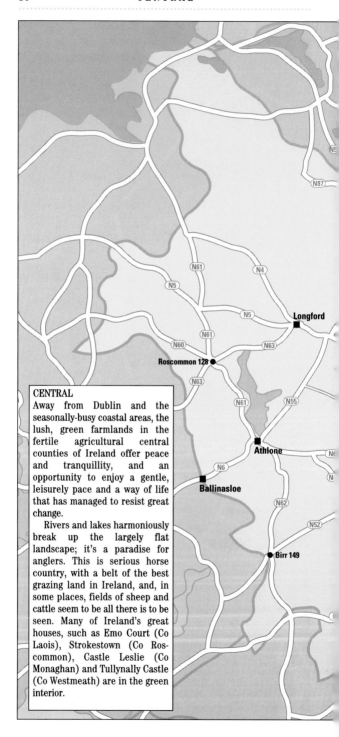

CENTRAL

Away from Dublin and the seasonally-busy coastal areas, the lush, green farmlands in the fertile agricultural central counties of Ireland offer peace and tranquillity, and an opportunity to enjoy a gentle, leisurely pace and a way of life that has managed to resist great change.

Rivers and lakes harmoniously break up the largely flat landscape; it's a paradise for anglers. This is serious horse country, with a belt of the best grazing land in Ireland, and, in some places, fields of sheep and cattle seem to be all there is to be seen. Many of Ireland's great houses, such as Emo Court (Co Laois), Strokestown (Co Roscommon), Castle Leslie (Co Monaghan) and Tullynally Castle (Co Westmeath) are in the green interior.

REPORTING TO THE GUIDE

Please write and tell us about your experiences of small hotels,
guest houses and inns, whether good or bad, whether listed in this
edition or not. As well as hotels in Venice & North-East Italy, we
are interested in charming small hotels in: Britain, Ireland, the rest
of Italy, France, Spain, Portugal, Germany, Switzerland and other
European countries, as well as the east and west coasts of the
United States.

The address to write to is:

> Charming Small Hotel Guides,
> Duncan Petersen Publishing Ltd,
> 31 Ceylon Road,
> London, W14 OPY
> England.

Checklist
Please use a separate sheet of paper for each report; include your
name, address and telephone number on each sheet.
  Your reports are particularly welcome if they are typed and
organized under the following headings:

> Name of establishment
> Town or village
> Full address and postcode
> Telephone number
> Time and duration of visit
> The building and setting
> Public rooms
> Bedrooms and bathrooms
> Standards of maintenance, housekeeping
> Standards of comfort and decoration
> Atmosphere, welcome and service
> Food
> Value for money

We assume that in writing you have no objection to your views
being published unpaid, either verbatim or in an edited version.
Names of major outside contributors are acknowledged in the
guide, at the editor's discretion.

Co Donegal

ARDARA

THE GREEN GATE
~ COTTAGE BED-AND-BREAKFAST ~

The Green Gate, Ardvally, Ardara, Co Donegal
TEL 075 41546

THIS LITTLE PLACE, a tiny farmhouse with stone outbuildings, owned and converted by a Frenchman who came to Donegal 11 years ago to write about "life, love and death", is bursting with charm. The book never got finished, but Paul Chatenoud, who left behind his musical bookshop and flat in Paris for a wilder existence on the top of a hill overlooking the Atlantic, has created what must be the most beautiful small B & B in Ireland. So much love and care has gone into this enterprise; he's done most of it with his own hands, from thatching the cottage roof to plumbing and whitewashing the four guest rooms. Simple they may be, but he thinks of everything: hot water bottles, a map in each room, and a bath in which you can rest your head back and gaze out of the window at the sky and the sea. His garden is filled with primroses, fuchsia and small birds, and he has planted hundreds, if not thousands, of orange montbretia up the lane. Breakfast is taken *chez lui*; in his own cosy kitchen he serves coffee/tea, cornflakes, bacon, eggs, sausage, toast and home-made jam – any time before 2 pm. And you get his delightful company. An English composer came for a night and was still there a week later. 'A treasure' says an entry in the visitor's book.

~

NEARBY Ardara (for tweed); Glenveagh National Park.
LOCATION a mile (1.6 km) from Ardara, up a hill; parking available
MEALS breakfast
PRICES £20 pp in thatched barn; £25 pp in cottage; breakfast included
ROOMS 4; 2 double, 2 with double bed and 1 single bed; all with bath and shower
FACILITIES garden, terrace
CREDIT CARDS none; cash or cheque taken
CHILDREN welcome
DISABLED possible
PETS welcome; to be kept in room
CLOSED never
PROPRIETOR Paul Chatenoud

CO ARMAGH

ARMAGH

DEAN'S HILL
~ TOWN GUEST-HOUSE ~

College Hill, Armagh, Co Armagh BT61 9DF
TEL/FAX 028 3752 4923

THERE HAVE BEEN Armstrongs in this lovely Georgian house in the ecclesiastical city of Armagh since 1870. It was built for the cathedral's dean in 1760 and, although the setting is rural, is only ten minutes walk from the historical centre of Armagh. A stone gatehouse on the road draws visitors up the long, gently curving driveway leading through green, daffodil-strewn fields, with mature trees and a large Cedar of Lebanon in the rambling garden. Inside, the welcoming, easy-going house attractively wears its patina of age, with what our inspector (most enthusiastically) describes as 'gorgeous' antique furniture, paintings and prints. Some of the tall, sash windows still carry their original glass, there are long white shutters and old floorboards covered with slightly worn carpets. Rugs are thrown over the easy chairs in the comfortable, relaxed sitting-room and the huge bedrooms are wonderfully old-fashioned and elegant. One has a single brass bedstead, and plenty of pictures hung, slightly crookedly, on the walls; another has dusky pink curtains and a wallpaper of climbing roses. The bathrooms, again, are old-fashioned, with pretty papers, prints and washstands. For breakfast, there is home-made jam and fresh eggs from the Armstrong farm.

~

NEARBY Armagh Planetarium; cathedral, museums.
LOCATION half a mile (0.8 km) from the town centre on A3 towards Craigavon – turn left at stone gate lodge; parking
MEALS breakfast
PRICES £25 pp in double; £19 in single; standard double £50; breakfast included
ROOMS 3; 1 four-poster with bath, 1 twin with bath, 1 single with private bath
FACILITIES gardens; tennis court, boules
CREDIT CARDS none
CHILDREN welcome
DISABLED not suitable
PETS with advance warning
CLOSED Christmas and New Year **PROPRIETORS** Jill and Edward Armstrong

Co Antrim

ASH-ROWAN LODGE
~ TOWN GUEST-HOUSE ~

12 Windsor Avenue, Belfast BT9 6EE
TEL 028 90661758 **FAX** 028 9066 3227

SAM AND EVELYN HAZLETT were restaurateurs and love good food and feeding people. The generous breakfasts at this comfortable, friendly, informal place keep you going throughout the day. We noted nine solid dishes on the menu, including mushrooms on toast, flambéed in sherry and with cream, kedgeree in ramekin dishes with cream and a 'hint of cumin', and variations on the Ulster Fry theme, depending on how faint-hearted you are feeling. The Hazletts' attractive Victorian family house stands in a tree-lined residential road and the welcoming hosts are especially popular with classical musicians making guest appearances with the Ulster Orchestra, most probably because of the homely atmosphere.

Each bedroom is decorated in an individual style: they are all comfortable and full of bits and pieces, as is the entire house. All have dressing gowns, and crisp Irish linens on beds. Some have antiques, some newer wicker furniture. Prettier, quite spacious, rooms at the top of the house have sloping attic ceilings, old white crocheted bedspreads, armchairs, plants, mixed colours. There are plenty of family 'things' in corridors and on landings: books, ornaments, a bird cage, old mirrors and porcelain, and dried flowers. A conservatory extension was being planned when we visited; it may now already be built and nicely filling up with 'things'.

~

NEARBY Ulster Museum; Botanic Gardens; Queen's University.
LOCATION in residential street between the Malone and Lisburn roads; 1 mile (1.6 km) S of the city centre; parking available
MEALS breakfast, dinner on request **PRICES** per room; £46-£79; standard double £52; breakfast included; dinner from £25
ROOMS 5; 3 double/twin, 2 single, 3 with bath, 2 with shower; all with phone, tv, hairdrier, trouser press; safe on request **FACILITIES** sitting-room
CREDIT CARDS AE, MC, V **CHILDREN** over 12 **DISABLED** not suitable **PETS** not accepted
CLOSED 22 Dec to 6 Jan **PROPRIETORS** Sam and Evelyn Hazlett

Co Antrim

BELFAST

THE CRESCENT TOWNHOUSE
~ CITY HOTEL ~

13 Lower Crescent, Belfast BT7 1NR
TEL 028 9032 3349 **FAX** 028 9032 0646

THIS COMFORTABLE, discreet little 'townhouse' was opened in 1998 in what used to be the premises of a rather seedy hotel – it's right in the middle of the buzzing university district on tree- and shop-lined Botanic Avenue, where there are fashionable clubs, cafés, bars and restaurants. Smartly illuminated with up-lighting at night and painted bright green, the listed building has been given a complete makeover and the result is an intimate and stylish little place with a shiny, modern brasserie called Metro, and a bar with old Victorian pub mirrors, panelling, and 'snugs'. The interior is lavishly fitted out and special thought has been given to business people: fax, photocopying and secretarial services are available and there are table tops for papers, pcs and briefcases in the upstairs, panelled reception area, which also has leather sofas, armchairs and sober portraits on the walls.

Upstairs, it's much too attractive to be kept just for business: smart, Regency-striped wallpaper and Ralph Lauren fabrics in the comfortable bedrooms; sparkling bathrooms with Victorian roll-top baths, separate power showers, bath robes and fluffy towels. Suites have canopied beds, some are sombre and masculine; standard rooms – looking like rooms in country houses – are lighter. Nine more rooms are on the way. Night porter.

~

NEARBY Queen's University; city centre, 1 mile (1.6 km); Ulster Museum.
LOCATION on Botanic Avenue, in busy university district, 1 mile S of city centre; no parking available
MEALS breakfast, lunch, dinner
PRICES rooms £90-£110; standard double £90; single £70; breakfast included; lunch £12; dinner £20 **ROOMS** 20; 14 double (4 twin), 6 suites; all with bath and shower; all rooms with phone, tv, radio, minibar, hairdrier, trouser press, CD player; safe in reception **FACILITIES** sauna, steam room; restaurant, bar; lift
CREDIT CARDS all major **CHILDREN** accepted **DISABLED** possible **PETS** not accepted
CLOSED Christmas; 11-13 July **PROPRIETOR** Matthew McAllister

Co Antrim

BELFAST

GREENWOOD HOUSE
~ TOWN GUEST-HOUSE ~

25 Park Road, Belfast, Co Antrim BT7 2FW
TEL 028 9020 2525 **FAX** 028 9020 2530
E-MAIL greenwood.house@virgin.net

JUST OFF THE (infamous) Ormeau Road, on a quiet tree-lined residential street, this is a double-fronted, red brick Victorian house in a small garden behind a privet hedge. Until three years ago it was a retirement home, but a transformation has been brought about by the delightful young present owners, Jason and Mary Harris. 'What a welcome change from dark colours, frills and fussiness', observed our inspector. Downstairs, the old maplewood floors and original cornicing remain, but the decoration is Habitat-style, contemporary and fresh, with bright fabrics in primary colours and much wrought-ironwork. The dining-room – at the front – has wrought-iron tables and chairs made by local craftsmen, wrought-iron curtain rails, red and yellow curtains, a handsome old fireplace and modern prints on the walls. Jason makes breakfast; the menu is written up on a blackboard. The same bright theme continues upstairs: wrought-iron bedsteads, a navy-blue and green colour scheme, mirrors in smart black frames, light wood tables with black trim, 'open' wardrobes (or an iron frame enclosed by fabric). Bathrooms are very white. Some rooms are quite large; those at the front look out over a park. The house style is informal and cheerful.

~

NEARBY city centre.
LOCATION in residential area, a mile (1.6 km) south of city centre; parking
MEALS breakfast, dinner on request
PRICES rooms £35 single, £25 pp double; breakfast included; dinner £15
ROOMS 7; 5 doubles, 2 twin; 3 with bath, 2 with shower; 2 singles with shower; all with tv, radio, trouser press; hairdrier available
FACILITIES garden
CREDIT CARDS AE, MC, V
CHILDREN welcome; cot
DISABLED downstairs room
PETS not accepted
CLOSED Christmas week **PROPRIETORS** Jason and Mary Harris

Co Antrim

LISDARA HOUSE

~ TOWN GUEST-HOUSE ~

23 Derryvolgie Avenue, Malone Road, Belfast BT9 6FN
TEL/FAX 028 9068 1549
E-MAIL elisabeth@lisdara.freeserve.co.uk

ACADEMICS VISITING the nearby Queen's University stay here. Not only is it convenient, but Elisabeth Gillespie, a former teacher who has opened her family home to guests, has an original touch and is a delightful hostess. In a quiet, residential avenue, in a conservation area, her attractive, buttermilk-coloured Victorian house stands in a pretty garden, a little set back from the road. There is blue-and-green William Morris wallpaper in the hall and guests have two sitting-rooms to choose from; the smaller has a grand piano and a framed collection of Oriental ivory fans hanging on the wall. The breakfast- and drawing-room are interconnected; two little bay trees stand in the window and there are French doors out to the garden and lemon yellow curtains. A search through the bookshelves may find novels by Elisabeth's daughter, Emer. Bedrooms are all different. One has an old brass bed and gold stencilling – by the son of the house – on the walls. Another has old floorboards, a big four-poster, dusty pink striped wallpaper, and freestanding bathtub in the room itself. A twin room has patchwork quilts, a little wrought-iron fireplace, and old editions of children's books on the shelves. Beds are made up with embroidered white linens.

~

NEARBY city centre shops; Queen's University; Ulster Museum.
LOCATION on quiet, residential street, 2 miles (3 km) out of city centre; parking available
MEALS breakfast, dinner on request
PRICES rooms single £40; double £60; breakfast included; dinner £17.50
ROOMS 5; 4 double (1 twin), 1 single; 2 with bath, 3 with shower; all with tv, hairdrier; phone available
FACILITIES terrace, garden; 2 sitting-rooms
CREDIT CARDS MC, V **CHILDREN** if well behaved
DISABLED not suitable
PETS not accepted
CLOSED Christmas; New Year **PROPRIETOR** Elisabeth Gillespie

CO ANTRIM

BELFAST

THE MCCAUSLAND HOTEL

~ CITY HOTEL ~

34-38 Victoria Street, Belfast, Co Antrim BT1 3GH
TEL 028 9022 0200 **FAX** 028 9022 0220
E-MAIL info@mccauslandhotel.com

A LTHOUGH MUCH LARGER than any of our other recommendations, we have made an exception for this stylish, interesting new hotel in the central Laganside quarter of Belfast, which opened in December 1998. Once two Victorian seed warehouses belonging to rival firms, the listed Italianate building with ornate carved stonework on the facade has been rescued from dereliction and given a smart, sophisticated, contemporary interior. Ground floor public rooms have the original columns and high-beamed ceilings; the reception area positively glows, with light wood, pale, honey-coloured stone floors and subtle lighting. Lofty palm trees decorate the hotel's attractive Marco Polo café bar and the restaurant has light parquet flooring, tall black columns and arched windows. The spaces and the architectural features of these handsome old commercial buildings lend themselves pleasingly and naturally to a new use. Warm, muted colours are used for the business-like, comfortable bedrooms; larger rooms have sofas and armchairs; top rooms have city skyline views. All have CD players. Our inspector was very taken with the brightly-lit, black and white tiled bathrooms; shiny chrome fixtures and fluffy apricot-coloured towels. There are special rooms for women.

~

NEARBY major galleries, theatres, shopping; Waterfront Hall.
LOCATION in centre, NE of City Hall and on west bank of river. Parking nearby
Meals breakfast, lunch, dinner
PRICES rooms £130-£200; standard double £150, breakfast included; lunch £14.50; dinner £30.
ROOMS 61; 31 double/twin, 15 singles; all with bath, 5 with shower; all rooms with phone, tv, radio, hairdrier, trouser press, safe; 15 suites, all with bath and shower
FACILITIES restaurant, bar, conference facilities, sitting-room.
CREDIT CARDS AE, DC, MC, V
CHILDREN accepted
DISABLED 3 rooms with baths
PETS small **CLOSED** New Year; 24-28 Dec **PROPRIETOR** Joseph Hughes

Co Antrim

THE BUSHMILLS INN
~ CONVERTED COACHING INN ~

25 Main Street, Bushmills, Co Antrim BT57 8QA
TEL 028 2073 2339 **FAX** 028 2073 2048
E-MAIL bushmills@bestloved.com

IT IS DIFFICULT to believe that chickens once lived on the first floor when this charming little inn, only a mile from the Giant's Causeway, was going through hard times. All that changed in 1987 when the present owners spotted the potential of the building. The oldest part – now the restaurant – dates back to the early 17thC when the nearby Old Bushmills Distillery was granted the world's first licence to distil whiskey. The entrance, through an archway from the street into the courtyard, leads to the front door in a little whitewashed round tower. Almost the first thing to be seen, once inside, is a glowing turf fire, which is always lit. A series of attractive ground-floor rooms includes a small 'snug' – the original kitchen – with a roaring fire and old flagstones; the Victorian-style bar has gas lighting, leather chairs, dark wood panelling and a wooden floor. Bedrooms come in two varieties: older ones, furnished in comfortable cottage style are in the inn itself; newer ones in the Mill House extension – with river views – are larger, with natural wood panelling, rough white walls and their own sitting area. There are plenty of strategically-placed rocking chairs in which to savour a bedtime slug of one of the classic malts from up the road.

~

NEARBY Giant's Causeway; Glens of Antrim; golf at Royal Portrush.
LOCATION in main street of village on A2, 5 miles (8 km) E of Portrush; parking
Meals breakfast, lunch, dinner
Prices rooms £68-£118; standard double £88; breakfast included; lunch £8; dinner £21.85
ROOMS 32; 28 double (22 twin); 24 with bath, 26 with shower; 4 singles with shower; all with phone, tv; 22 with hairdrier, trouser press, computer socket
FACILITIES terrace, garden; bar, restaurant, sitting-rooms
CREDIT CARDS AE, MC
CHILDREN welcome **DISABLED** adapted bedroom **PETS** accepted; not in restaurant
CLOSED never **PROPRIETORS** Roy Bolton and Richard Wilson

Co Monaghan

CLONES

HILTON PARK
~ COUNTRY HOUSE ~

Clones, Co Monaghan
TEL 047 56007 **FAX** 047 56033
E-MAIL hiltonpk@indigo.ie

IN THE HIDDEN IRELAND group of country houses taking paying guests is Hilton Park – home of the Madden family since 1734 and remodelled in the Italianate manner in the 1870s. It is grand, beautiful, and most evocative of the great days of the Irish country house. Johnny Madden emerges out of his huge front door under the portico to greet guests and carries baggage into the hall and up the panelled staircase. A wizard with bacon, he prepares breakfast, which is served in the old servants' hall below stairs. He and his wife Lucy, a food writer and accomplished cook, are memorably delightful hosts. Many family stories are to be told about the guest bedrooms: one was Johnny's when he was a child. Little seems to have changed over the years. The wallpaper in the Blue Room, with a four-poster bed and stunning view down to the lake, was put up in 1830. On our visit, the lace curtains had just come out of a box opened for the first time since 1927. Next door, a roll-top bath, marble washstand, print of Landseer's *Hunters at Grass*, and the scent of jasmine from plants in pots arranged at the foot of the tall window, all add to the grace and charm. Lucy's dinner is by candlelight, with fresh produce from her organic garden.

~

NEARBY Castle Coole and Florence Court (National Trust); Armagh.
LOCATION 3 miles (5 km) S of Clones, near Clones Golf Club; in 500 acres of parkland, woods, lakes; parking
MEALS breakfast, dinner
PRICES rooms I£57.50 pp or I£67.50 pp; standard double I£115; breakfast included; dinner I£25
ROOMS 6; 5 double, 1 twin; all with bath; all rooms have hairdrier, electric blanket and hot water bottles
FACILITIES gardens with seats; games room; grand piano; pike and brown trout fishing; rods; boating on lake **CREDIT CARDS** AE, MC, V
CHILDREN over 7 by arrangement **DISABLED** not possible **PETS** by arrangement
CLOSED end Sept to end Mar **PROPRIETORS** Johnny and Lucy Madden

CO DONEGAL

DONEGAL

ST ERNAN'S HOUSE HOTEL

~ ISLAND HOTEL ~

St Ernan's Island, Donegal, Co Donegal
TEL 073 21065 **FAX** 073 22098
E-MAIL sainternans@tinet.ie **WEBSITE** www.sainternans.com

THIS SMALL SUGAR-PINK hotel on a wooded island caters for those who want peace and quiet and is tireless in striving for perfection. On a part of the Donegal coastline that has a natural serenity, the house was built in the 1820s by a nephew of the Duke of Wellington for his sick wife, who needed sea air to cure her of a debilitating cough. More recently a retirement home for clergy and a restaurant-with-rooms, it was bought in 1987 by banker Brian O'Dowd and his wife, Carmel, a teacher, who have gradually been restoring it to the country house it once was. The pursuit – and entrapment – of peace and quiet has produced a most pleasing and civilized result. And four star comfort. From almost every window there is a view of mesmerising, still water, and Carmel has filled the house with antiques, pictures and pretty fabrics. The most coveted bedroom is the cosy attic, with views down over water and trees. The tone of the place is immediately set by the fact that there are no tables or chairs for sitting outside. The dress code prohibits sandals and shorts; there's no TV downstairs, either. A leisurely five-course meal in the evening rounds off the day. "A strange little breed" says Mrs O'Dowd, affectionately, of the peace and quiet *aficionados*. Wise, too.

~

NEARBY Donegal Town, 2 miles (3 km); Sligo, 42 miles (67.5 km).
LOCATION 2 miles out of Donegal on the N15; follow signposts; parking
Meals breakfast, dinner
PRICES rooms I£73-I£89 pp; standard double I£158; breakfast included; dinner I£17-I£34.50
ROOMS 12; all double/twin; all with bath/shower, 3 with full shower; all with phone, tv, radio, hairdrier
FACILITIES gardens; woodland and shore walks
CREDIT CARDS MC, V
CHILDREN not under 6
DISABLED not possible **PETS** not accepted **CLOSED** 1 Jan to mid-Apr; end Oct to 31 Dec **PROPRIETORS** Brian and Carmel O'Dowd

Co Tyrone

Dungannon

Grange Lodge

~ Country house ~

Grange Road, Dungannon, Co Tyrone BT71 7EJ
Tel 028 8778 4212 **Fax** 028 8778 4313

Our reporter was enchanted by the setting – on a little hill in large and lovely gardens – of this rambling, ivy clad, Georgian house with later additions. But it is the Grange Lodge table that has won distinction and found it so many friends. Norah Brown, who is self-taught, has several awards for her outstandingly good cooking and she and her husband, Ralph, are relaxed, easy-going, welcoming hosts. Much of the fruit, vegetables and herbs she uses are homegrown and sometimes a second dining-room is opened up to outside groups looking for her special talent and dishes from her "best friend", the Aga. Admirers praise the ageless quality of her food and her sure touch; she says people have just forgotten what real home cooking is. Her husband has the happy task of bringing breakfast out from the kitchen: try Mrs Brown's porridge with brown sugar, cream and Bushmills whiskey, rhubarb compote, soda bread and Ulster grill with potato cake. The sitting-room – there's a 'den' with TV, too – is immaculate, in elegant dark colours; most surfaces are crammed with ornaments, family photos, pewter and plates. Upstairs, ivy pushes at the window panes of the bedrooms. Some of Mrs Brown's biscuits are always to be found on the hospitality tray.

~

Nearby Tyrone; Ulster American Folk Park
Location in countryside 3 miles (5 km) S of Dungannon off the A 29 to Armagh; parking available
Meals breakfast, dinner
Prices rooms £49 single; £69 pp double/twin; breakfast included; dinner from £22
Rooms 5; 3 doubles, 1 twin, 1 single; 1 with bath, 1 with hip-bath, 3 with shower; all with phone, tv, hairdrier, tea/coffee making facilities
Facilities sitting-rooms; gardens
Credit cards MC, V
Children over 12 **Disabled** not possible **Pets** welcome outside
Closed 20 Dec to 1 Feb **Proprietors** Norah and Ralph Brown

Co Donegal

CASTLE MURRAY HOUSE
~ COUNTRY RESTAURANT WITH ROOMS ~

St John's Point, Dunkineely, Co Donegal
TEL 073 37022 **FAX** 073 37330

ON OUR VISIT, this, despite all the accolades, was up for sale. The dynamic, gifted young couple, Claire Delcros and her chef husband, Thierry, who turned a small farmhouse into a thriving business with a considerable reputation, were planning to return to France. The longer it takes, the better it will be for anyone who has not yet enjoyed this charming little place. The setting could be called magical. In front of the hotel, bright green fields with low, drystone walls run down to the sea and a small ruined castle on the point is illuminated as night falls. Across the bay, the sun goes down over the Slieve League, the highest sea cliffs in Europe. Thierry's very French restaurant has the best food in the area, beams, flagged floor, exposed stone walls, lobsters pottering about in a tank by the raised, open fire, and – a typical Mme Delcros touch – Donegal tweed curtains. Up a pine staircase, bedrooms are basic, and remind one of any small French hotel. Our inspector noted matching curtains, bedspread and window seat cushions in *eau-de-nil* checks, a print of a Normandy seaside resort, and one rough wall and another in a rose-strewn paper. Verdant foliage rampages through the small enclosed terrace downstairs; game birds adorn the bar.

~

NEARBY Donegal.
LOCATION a mile (1.6 km) off the main N56 from Donegal to Killybegs, signposted in Dunkineely; parking
MEALS breakfast, dinner
PRICES rooms I£33 pp; standard double I£60; breakfast included; dinner from I£18
ROOMS 10 (9 with sea view); 5 double, 5 twin; 2 with bath, 2 with shower; all with phone, tv, hairdrier, tea/coffee making facilities
FACILITIES garden, terrace; bar
CREDIT CARDS MC, V
CHILDREN welcome **DISABLED** not possible **PETS** small dogs in rooms
CLOSED end Jan to beg Feb **PROPRIETORS** Claire and Thierry Delcros

Co Donegal

Lough Eske

Ardnamona

~ Country house ~

Lough Eske, Co Donegal
Tel 073 22650 **Fax** 073 22819
E-mail ardnamona@tempoweb.com

HALF-HIDDEN on a jungly hillside of rhododendrons and azaleas – planted in the 1880s and now a 40-acre National Heritage Garden – and on the shores of Lough Eske, with the Blue Stack mountains in the distance, this is a hauntingly romantic, beautiful place. Amabel Clarke, who worked as a Russian interpreter in London, and her husband, Kieran, a piano tuner, welcome guests to their gabled Victorian house, filled with charming rooms and the aroma of delicious home cooking wafting from the kitchen. The interiors are a pleasure: a leafy conservatory with bamboo furniture looks over the lake; green sofas, velvet curtains, tartan *chaise longue* and a wood fire in the sitting-room; upstairs, painted floorboards, faded pinks and mauves, patchwork quilts, white curtains and architectural prints. There are Sotheby's Reviews to read; walks through the restored gardens, once overgrown and neglected, and rescued by the Clarkes – best in April and May; fresh eggs from the free-range chickens for breakfast; leisurely evenings, talking, in front of the fire. Amabel has recently discovered an Italian delicatessen in Belfast that delivers. And, sometimes, across the stable yard, comes the sound of Kieran playing his piano that once belonged to Padarewski.

~

Nearby Donegal, 6 miles (10 km).
Location in own extensive lakeside grounds off the N15 from Donegal to Letterkenny; parking
Meals breakfast, dinner
Prices rooms I£40pp–I£47 pp; standard double I£80; breakfast included; dinner I£20
Rooms 6; 4 double, 2 twin; 3 with bathroom attached, 3 with bathroom next door; all with hairdrier
Facilities sitting-room; gardens
Credit cards AE, MC, V
Children welcome **Disabled** not possible **Pets** allowed outside
Closed Christmas Day **Proprietors** Kieran and Amabel Clarke

Co Donegal

Lough Eske

HARVEY'S POINT
~ COUNTRY HOTEL AND RESTAURANT ~

Lough Eske, Donegal Town, Co Donegal
Tel 073 22208 **Fax** 073 22352

THE LARGE CAR PARK and new gates are less than charming. But press on beyond these to find a warm and friendly little sanctuary among the trees by the lakeside, where you will eat exceptionally well and be looked after in a kindly, courteous, professional manner. The parking is for the functions and hugely popular Sunday carvery-style lunches, but the bedrooms – some have little sitting-rooms – are in a secluded, quiet, private, single-storey lodge on the shore by the still waters of the lake. All 'executive' rooms have repro four-posters and lake or mountain view; 'superior' rooms are slightly Swiss in flavour, with wooden floors and fresh white bed linen. All rooms have their own door on to the covered walkway around the lodge, and double-glazed windows for a restful night. The hotel keeps its own little fleet of ducks and geese that dabble in the shallow waters on the edge of the lake, and the waterside lawns, right outside the lodge, are a delightful place to sit and watch the fish jumping. Harvey's Point makes an ideal touring base, but there is plenty to do on the premises, such as fishing from the jetty, or tennis. When we visited, stables had been built and horses were about to arrive, as owner Deirdre McGloin has always wanted to provide riding for guests. The lake is a magical spot. The restaurant collects awards.

~

Nearby Donegal; Galway; Connemara; golf.
Location in gardens and grounds, 4 miles (6 km) out of Donegal Town, on Lough Eske Drive; with parking
Meals breakfast, lunch, dinner
Prices rooms; from I£49-I£55pp; standard double I£100; breakfast included; lunch from I£12.50; dinner I£28 **Rooms** 16; all double/twin with bath and shower; all rooms with phone, tv, radio, minibar, hairdrier; some with trouser press
Facilities gardens; tennis, fishing, riding
Credit cards all major **Children** accepted, but not in restaurant after 6pm
Disabled possible **Pets** welcome **Closed** end Nov to beg Mar (open weekends, Christmas, New Year) **Proprietor/Manager** Deirde McGloin

CO DOWN

THE NARROWS

~ SEASIDE GUEST-HOUSE ~

8 Shore Road, Portaferry, Co Down BT22 1JY
TEL 028 4272 8148 **FAX** 028 4272 8105
E-MAIL reservations@narrows.co.uk

THIS IS AN ARCHITECTURAL TREAT. Not only that: its seafront position in a pretty fishing village on the tip of the beautiful Ards peninsula; its sunny, bright rooms with views over the water; and its prices, which take some beating, all make this a gem. Around an 18thC courtyard, owner-brothers Will and James Brown have restored and extended their father's family house with the help of architect, Rachel Bevan. The result is an exciting, airy, pleasing combination of old and new. The 13 bedrooms, all named after islands in Strangford Lough, have windows looking over boats and the new yacht pontoon. Decoration is simple, with white walls, coconut matting, natural wood floors, pine furniture and white-tiled bathrooms. Rooms in the older building have aged timber beams; all have good beds and power showers. The ground floor restaurant is a bright, functional room, with wood floors, sponged terracotta-coloured walls and bare wood tables, serving delicious Modern Irish food, with local seafood, such as Portaferry mussels, smoked salmon, and sea bass. Organic vegetables and herbs come from the garden. The odd well-placed colourful piece of hand-weaving, painting or photograph hangs on the walls. Moorings available.

~

NEARBY Exploris Aquarium; Mount Stewart (National Trust); golf.
LOCATION on seafront in centre of town; parking for 4/5 cars
MEALS breakfast, lunch, dinner
PRICES rooms £39pp; standard double £78; breakfast included; lunch £10; dinner £20
ROOMS 13; 12 double/twin, 1 single; 3 with bath, 10 with shower; all with phone, tv
FACILITIES garden, terrace, sauna; restaurant, sitting-room; lift
CREDIT CARDS AE, MC, V
CHILDREN welcome; cot
DISABLED 8 accessible rooms; lift **PETS** accepted with own bedding
CLOSED 2 weeks in Feb **PROPRIETORS** Will and James Brown

Co Donegal

RATHMULLAN

RATHMULLAN HOUSE
~ COUNTRY HOUSE HOTEL ~

Rathmullan, Letterkenny, Co Donegal
Tel 074 58188 **Fax** 074 58200
E-mail rathhse@iol.ie

THERE'S NOT MUCH missing at Rathmullan House: warm hospitality; four-star comfort; a lovely setting in acres of gardens with paths winding through the trees down to a sandy beach on Lough Swilly and views of mountains across the water. The mornings here, even misty ones, are full of promise: there's much to do. A walk along the shore; a swim in the heated pool; a game of tennis; watch the rabbits on the lawn; read a book in front of the log fire in any of the three delightful sitting-rooms. There are no keys to the bedrooms (they may be locked from the inside) and although Rathmullan House – once the home of a Belfast banking family - grows and grows, it still retains an alluring intimacy and friendliness which tempts guests back again and again. Some rooms in the rambling old house have bay windows and lough views; some have four-posters; those in the newish annexe above the pool have large plate glass windows opening on to balconies. The conservatory dining-room is tented, which gives every meal, even breakfast, a sense of occasion. Owners Bob and Robin Wheeler's son, Mark, has inherited their gift for making guests feel at home and is a natural host, always available to help and to talk. (Pity about the unsightly rash of holiday cottages.)

~

NEARBY "Flight of the Earls" Heritage Centre; Glenveagh National Park.
LOCATION in own grounds, on shores of Lough Swilly; with parking
MEALS breakfast, lunch, dinner
PRICES rooms I£45pp-I£67.50pp; standard double I£110; breakfast included; lunch from I£5; dinner I£30.25
ROOMS 24; 11 suites, 8 superiors, 5 standards; 11 twins, 13 double (3 family); all with bath and shower; all with phone, tv, hairdrier
FACILITIES terraces, garden, heated pool; steam room, sauna; tennis; beautician
CREDIT CARDS AE, DC, MC, V
CHILDREN welcome
DISABLED special rooms
PETS not accepted **CLOSED** never **PROPRIETORS** Bob and Robin Wheeler

CO LONDONDERRY

UPPERLANDS

ARDTARA
~ GUEST-HOUSE ~

8 Gorteade Road, Upperlands, Co Londonderry BT46 5SA
TEL 028 7964 4490 **FAX** 028 7964 5080

THIS SEVERE, grey Victorian house – built in 1856 for one of the Clark family, owners of the linen mill in the village – was saved from dereliction and given a new life by Maebeth Fenton, who works for the Northern Ireland Tourist Board in New York. Ardtara means 'the house on the hill'. Open to guests now for five years, it is luxuriously comfortable and garlanded with awards. The meticulous conversion has been done with the style befitting a house with fairly grand pretensions. Many original features, such as fireplaces and plasterwork, have been preserved, and the house is filled with antiques and fabrics carefully chosen to continue the Victorian theme. The effect is warm, glowing and full of interest. The panelled ladies' room downstairs, for example, has the original double basin. Upstairs, the rooms are spacious, with working fireplaces. Bathrooms, in our inspector's words, are 'wonderful': varnished wood floors; two with fireplaces; one with a Victorian hip-bath; another bath has claw feet; brass fittings; old washstands; pretty paper; fresh flowers. Power showers, fluffy white towels and bathrobes make them places to linger in and to enjoy. The drawing-room is bright and sunny; the restaurant has a glass skylight and original hunting scene frieze.

NEARBY Royal Portrush golf course, 20 miles (32 km); Giant's Causeway, 30 miles (48 km).
LOCATION 3 miles N of Maghera on B75 (off A29); signposted in village; with parking
Meals breakfast, lunch, dinner
PRICES rooms £80-£120; standard doubles £100; breakfast included; lunch £14.50; dinner £22.50
ROOMS 8; all double/twin; all with bath and shower; all with phone, tv, radio, hairdrier; safe in reception **FACILITIES** 2 sitting-rooms, restaurant; gardens; tennis court, golf tee; conservatory **CREDIT CARDS** all major **CHILDREN** well-behaved welcome **DISABLED** not suitable **PETS** accepted **CLOSED** 25 and 26 Dec
PROPRIETOR Maebeth Fenton

Co Tipperary

AGLISH

BALLYCORMAC HOUSE

~ CONVERTED FARMHOUSE ~

Aglish, Borrisokane, Co Tipperary
TEL 067 21129 **FAX** 067 21200

SET AMID NORTH TIPPERARY FARMLAND, almost exactly in the middle of Ireland, this is a 300-year-old-farmhouse which has long been well known as a guest house, but which was taken over from the previous occupants in 1994 by an energetic American couple, Herbert and Christine Quigley. It's ideal for guests who simply wish to relax, or small groups who want to take advantage of their specialist holidays based on riding, fox-hunting, golfing, fishing and shooting. We learned, on going to press, that the Quigleys have left, so readers' reports would be especially welcome.

The Quigleys upgraded the pretty but compact house, creating a warm and cosy retreat. There are log fires in winter, and in summer guests can see the organic herb, fruit and vegetable gardens which provide produce for meals. And this is where the Quigleys' real prowess lay. Herb was a superb baker, and so breakfast might feature traditional Irish soda bread, or his own version of *pain au chocolat*, chocolate cherry soda bread, while dinner at the communal table might be accompanied by anything from home-made Swedish *limpa* to Indian *naan*. Let's hope that the new owners can maintain this quality and individuality.

~

NEARBY Terryglass, 3 miles (4.5 km); Birr, 7 miles (11 km).
LOCATION in 2 acres of gardens, 0.5 mile (1 km) north of Borrisokane, signposted on right; ample car parking
MEALS breakfast, picnic lunch on request, dinner; wine licence
PRICES B&B I£35-I£40; dinner weekdays I£20, weekends I£24
ROOMS 5; 3 double, 1 suite, 1 single; all with bath; all rooms have central heating
FACILITIES sitting-room, dining- room; garden
CREDIT CARDS MC, V
CHILDREN welcome over 6 years
DISABLED access difficult **PETS** accepted but not in rooms; lodging available
CLOSED never **PROPRIETOR** John Lang

Co Mayo

BALLINA (Co Mayo)

MOUNT FALCON CASTLE
∼ COUNTRY HOUSE ∼

Ballina, Co Mayo
TEL 096 21172 or 70811 **Fax** 096 71517
E-MAIL mfsalmon@iol.ie

THIS GREY STONE Victorian house is not a castle at all - more Scottish baronial. Owner Constance Aldridge thinks she may have been entertaining guests here for longer than anyone else in the country - since way back in the 1930s. This is one of the great fishing houses of Ireland; it has its own stretch of the Moy, one of the most prolific salmon rivers in Europe, and nearby Loughs Conn and Cullen offer some of the best brown trout fishing. It is also one of the great character houses: friendly and traditional, where things continue to be done much as they always have been in the past. There are bowls of water for dogs in the front hall; good old-fashioned baths for weary fishermen; and what a leading food critic describes as one of the 'more singular dining experiences'. Known for her wit, Mrs Aldridge, when she can, still sits at the head of a long table, summoning each course – dinner is a hearty six-course affair – with a little bell. It is "plain cooking" she says: plenty of fish and game; vegetables and fruit come from the kitchen garden. She loves having children to stay; pony rides can be arranged. Her grandson, Steven, now helps, but nothing much changes. "We like to say yes to everything if we can", she says. It is a winning formula.
∼

NEARBY Foxford Woollen Mills; Downpatrick Head; Knock.
LOCATION on 100-acre estate, 4 miles (6 km) from Ballina on the N26 to Foxford; parking available
MEALS breakfast, picnic lunch, dinner
PRICES rooms I£35-I£60pp; standard doubles I£120; breakfast included; lunch I£7; dinner I£20
ROOMS 10; 6 superior double/twin, 2 standard twin, 2 single; all with bathroom; all with phone; hairdrier on request
FACILITIES garden; woodland walks, fishing
CREDIT CARDS AE, DC, MC, V
CHILDREN welcome; high tea **DISABLED** not possible **PETS** dogs welcome
CLOSED 10 days at Christmas **PROPRIETOR** Mrs Constance Aldridge

CO TIPPERARY

WATERMAN'S LODGE
~ VILLAGE HOTEL ~

Ballina, Killaloe, Co Tipperary
TEL 061 376333 **FAX** 061 375445
E-MAIL info@watermanslodge.ie

THIS IS CALLED A 'COUNTRY HOUSE', but is really more of a bungalow converted into a smart, pink, tailored little hotel by the previous owner, who, to make a restaurant, covered over the inner courtyard with skylights. New owner, Marcus McMahon, a Limerick businessman, has added a conservatory bar at one end of the building, and there may be more bedrooms soon, too. The sitting-room windows look down over meadows of grazing cattle to boats on the River Shannon and, beyond, to the painted terraced houses of Killaloe on the other side of the bridge. What is charming is the small and intimate scale of the house; so far, this has not been spoiled by renovations. An interior designer from Cork has added inspired touches like needlework cushions and new linen in the comfortable, pretty bedrooms. The hall entrance has a maple floor and the use of glassed-in French doors, contemporary pictures, pale, natural matting and indoor plants gives a fresh, light, uplifting effect to the public areas. The restaurant dining-room is most inviting, with pink walls and tongue-and-groove panelling. A couple of neat potted bay trees stand at attention outside the front door; there are plans afoot for landscaping the garden. Tom Reilly is the obliging general manager.

~

NEARBY Lough Derg; Limerick, 20 miles (32 km); Shannon airport, 23 miles (37 km).
LOCATION in riverside village, on the Shannon; parking available
MEALS breakfast, bar lunch; dinner
PRICES rooms I£55-I£65pp; standard double I£110; breakfast included; lunch from I£7; dinner I£28.50
ROOMS 11; 7 double, 3 twin, 1 single; 9 with bath, 2 with shower only; all with phone, tv, radio, hairdrier
FACILITIES garden, terrace; sitting-room, restaurant
CREDIT CARDS AE, MC, V
CHILDREN welcome; cot; high chair **DISABLED** possible **PETS** if well-behaved
CLOSED 20 Dec to 10 Feb **PROPRIETOR** Marcus McMahon

CO TIPPERARY

BALLINDERRY

GURTHALOUGHA HOUSE
～ COUNTRY HOUSE HOTEL ～

Ballinderry, Nenagh, Co Tipperary
TEL 067 22080 **FAX** 067 22154

BY THE TIME YOU REACH the end of the mile-long drive which twists and turns through the forest on the way to this hotel beside Lough Derg, it is easy to believe that you have travelled back to an altogether more peaceful and graceful era. Sadly, Michael and Bessie Wilkinson are leaving Gurthalougha House, after seventeen years here, but with assurances that the civilized and serene atmosphere they created will be retained by new owner, Anne Pettit.

The spacious high-ceilinged public rooms have plenty of pictures and antiques, but the search for style has not got in the way of comfort. The long, well-lit sitting-room, with its two open fireplaces and big cosy armchairs, is notably relaxed, while the enormous panelled library has a substantial collection of books about the locality. This restraint continues through into the bedrooms, which are spacious and carefully (though fairly sparsely) furnished, with no modern trimmings.

A set menu each evening, which may include locally-caught pike and smoked eel. A recent visitor praised the food, and we welcome further reports.

～

NEARBY Birr Castle gardens, 12 miles (19 km); Birr Castle gardens, 12 miles (19 km); Limerick.
LOCATION just W of village, 10 miles (16 km) N of Nenagh off L152; in 100-acre woodland on lakeside, with ample car parking
MEALS full breakfast, snack (or packed) lunch, dinner; wine licence (though other drinks available)
PRICES B&B I£32-I£38; dinner I£15; bargain breaks
ROOMS 8; 8 double, 6 with bath, 2 with shower; all rooms have central heating, phone
FACILITIES dining-room, sitting-room, library; table tennis, croquet, tennis, rowing-boats **CREDIT CARDS** AE, MC, V **CHILDREN** accepted, if well-behaved; high tea available **DISABLED** access not easy – 2 sets of steps on ground floor
PETS accepted if well-behaved **CLOSED** Christmas, Feb **PROPRIETOR** Anne Pettit

CO GALWAY

ERRISEASK HOUSE HOTEL

~ COUNTRY HOTEL ~

Ballyconneely, Co Galway
TEL 095 23553 **FAX** 095 23639
E-MAIL erriseask@connemara-ireland.com

WITH ITS OWN BEACH and surrounded by the windswept, wild beauty of the Connemara countryside, this is the perfect place for those who want to get away. And eat well while on the run. Because of the isolated position - we spent some time trying to find it - it is very much a sand-in-your-shoes summer place, with lazy days and easy living laid on by the brothers Matz. Christian is in charge of front of house; Stefan, the chef, has made something of a name for himself as one of the best cooks in Ireland. So, there is the feeling around that you must catch him while you can, because he's clearly destined for great things. The kitchen here is busy, serious, and professional; the formal restaurant is open to non-residents. The 'foodies' come from far and wide; there is a *Menu Degustation*. The hotel itself is pretty basic and functional, with much pine furniture. There are five stunning split-level rooms, with spiral staircases leading up to a platform and views of the sea. Nothing fancy. Practical and minimal, they make you want to unpack swiftly, dig in, and take advantage of all the good, simple, unpretentious treats offered here: Stefan's Connemara lamb; white coral beaches; glorious West Coast sunsets; moonlight over Mannin Bay.

~

NEARBY Connemara National Park; Kylemore Abbey; Clifden, 6 miles (10 km).
LOCATION in own gardens and grounds by seashore; parking available
MEALS breakfast, dinner
PRICES rooms I£40.50-I£48.50pp; standard double I£81; breakfast included; dinner I£19.50-I£35
ROOMS 12; 6 doubles, 4 twins, 1 single, 1 family with double bed and 2 singles; 5 with bath and shower, 7 with shower; all with phone, hairdrier; tv on request
FACILITIES garden, terraces
CREDIT CARDS AE, DC, MC, V
CHILDREN not in dining-room; no special facilities
DISABLED not possible
PETS not accepted **CLOSED** end Oct to Easter **PROPRIETOR** Christian Matz

Co Sligo

TEMPLE HOUSE
~ COUNTRY HOUSE ~

Ballymote, Co Sligo
TEL 071 83329 **FAX** 071 83808
E-MAIL accom@templehouse.ie

IS THIS A DREAM? It begins as you enter the gates of what is a gentle, gracious world of its own. In parkland filled with fat sheep, this is a whopper of a Georgian mansion, the home of the Percevals since 1665. Much of what you see was refurbished in 1864; electricity was not put in until 1962. To be overcome by awe and wonder would be easy were it not for the charm and kindness of Sandy Perceval (he is allergic to perfumed products and sprays, so please avoid use) and his wife, Debonnaire (or Deb). They want the house to be enjoyed. The two-storey vestibule is so enormous that Deb waits until guests have absorbed it before she speaks: 'There's no conversation when they arrive, they are usually speechless', she says. Bedrooms, with marble fireplaces and much of their original Victorian furniture, seem to be the size of football pitches – one is called the 'half acre'. Bathrooms have been put into what used to be dressing-rooms. As shadows fall, you can take a walk to the ruins of a 13thC Knights Templar castle and a Tudor house down by the lake. The family silver comes out for dinner; delicious dishes and freshly-baked bread emerge from Deb's all-electric kitchen which, of course, is vast. Big breakfasts.

~

NEARBY Sligo, 12 miles (19 km); Yeats Country; Lissadell House.
LOCATION on 1,000-acre estate, 4 miles (6 km) from Ballymote; parking available
MEALS breakfast, dinner
PRICES rooms I£42-I£45pp; standard double I£90; breakfast included; dinner I£19
ROOMS 5; 2 double, 2 twin (1 double and 1 single), 1 single; 2 with bath, 3 with shower; all with hairdrier
FACILITIES garden; woodland, lake fishing, boat
CREDIT CARDS AE, MC, V
CHILDREN welcome; high tea in kitchen for under-5s
DISABLED not possible
PETS dogs on leads (sheep); sleep in car
CLOSED 30 Nov to 1 Apr
PROPRIETORS Sandy and Deb Perceval

Co Galway

CAHERLISTRANE

LISDONAGH HOUSE
~ COUNTRY HOUSE ~

Caherlistrane, Co Galway
TEL 093 31163 **FAX** 093 31528
E-MAIL lisdonagh@iol.ie

HORSES GRAZE BY THE LAKE in front of this early Georgian house in the heart of the famous Galway hunting country – flat with drystone walls. Indeed, it used to belong to a maiden lady of the kind described as a 'colourful character', who rode to hounds and chased off intruders with a shotgun. Her antics may be read about in the enticing, cosy, basement 'den', where glowing fire, books and music are thoughtfully provided for guests, along with a help-yourself tray of various tipples and an Honesty Book. Extensively refurbished by current owners, John and Finola Cooke, over the last few years, the house has been refloored and filled with antiques, mainly found in England. Bedrooms are named after Irish writers; each one is different. Our inspector's room – with original shutters to fit the curved windows – had cream paintwork, a pretty French bed and chairs and a small bathroom with shower. The oval hallway – entered through the fanlighted front door – is quite remarkable, with frescoes of Ionic pillars and figures in grisaille of the Four Virtues – Valour, Justice, Chastity and Beauty – painted in 1790. A South African chef was cooking when we visited; delectable fresh breads come from the Aga. The kitchen garden is next for restoration.

~

NEARBY Galway; Sligo; Yeats Country; Kylemore Abbey.
LOCATION in countryside, 1 mile (1.5 km) from village of Caherlistrane; parking available
MEALS breakfast, lunch
PRICES rooms I£47-I£57pp; standard double I£114; breakfast included; dinner I£25
ROOMS 10; 5 double, 5 twin; 7 with bath, 3 with shower; all with phone, tv, video, radio, hairdrier; tea/coffee making facilities
FACILITIES lake fishing, boat, riding, woodland walks
CREDIT CARDS AE, MC, V
CHILDREN welcome **DISABLED** downstairs room **PETS** not in house; kennel
CLOSED 8 Dec to mid-Feb **PROPRIETORS** John and Finola Cooke

CO GALWAY

CASHEL BAY

ZETLAND HOUSE HOTEL

~ COUNTRY HOUSE HOTEL ~

Cashel Bay, Co Galway
TEL 095 31111 **FAX** 095 31117
E-MAIL zetland@iol.ie

THE BROCHURE HAS PRETTY PICTURES of a little table laid with a pink cloth and sunlight slanting through windows into antique-filled rooms. But we think it is the charming Prendergast family that brings regulars back again and again for more of the Zetland House experience. The setting happens to be spectacular, in an area of outstanding natural beauty, with views over Cashel Bay. Built in the early 19thC as a shooting lodge, the hotel is named after the Earl of Zetland, who was a frequent visitor. Mona Prendergast and her husband, John, who trained at the Ritz in Paris, have been joined by their children: son Ruaidhri has come home after working in Lille in France; daughter Cliodhna is in the kitchen. No wonder they've won an AA Care and Courtesy Award. Nothing is too much trouble. Ask Mona about the area, and she hurries off to find for you a copy of a map she has had printed up, so she can show you the best route to take or where to shop in Galway. Bedrooms are delightful. The Green Room has its own door to the garden, fresh, green trellis wallpaper, a marble washstand, and Edward Lear's Book of Nonsense on the bedside table. A fire is lit every morning in one of the sitting-rooms; there's an eye-catching collection of china plates.

~

NEARBY Aran Islands; Connemara National Park; Clifden, 14 miles (22.5 km).
LOCATION in gardens overlooking Cashel Bay, on N340 to Roundstone from Galway; parking available
MEALS breakfast, lunch, dinner
PRICES rooms I£59.50-I£79.50pp; standard double I£119; breakfast included; lunch I£7.50; dinner I£29.50
ROOMS 20; 10 double; 10 twin; 9 with bath, 1 with shower; all with phone, tv, radio, hairdrier
FACILITIES tennis court; snooker room; garden; shooting, fishing
CREDIT CARDS AE, DC, MC, V **CHILDREN** welcome **DISABLED** ground-floor room
PETS dogs with baskets permitted in bedrooms **CLOSED** 1 Nov to Easter
PROPRIETORS John and Mona Prendergast

Co Sligo

CASTLEBALDWIN

CROMLEACH LODGE
~ RESTAURANT WITH ROOMS ~

Castlebaldwin, Boyle, Co Sligo
TEL 071 65155 **FAX** 071 65455
E-MAIL cromleac@iol.ie

A SMALL MIRACLE: from modest beginnings as a bungalow with B & B for fishermen on Christy Tighe's family farm overlooking Lough Arrow, this unique little place has a string of coveted awards to its name. The modern design may not suit all tastes, but the Tighes were determined it should not be a blot on the green and beautiful landscape. So the building is long and low, under a slate roof, and looks as if it has grown out of the hillside. Ever-changing skies, still waters of the lake, cattle in the fields and blue-grey hills in the distance have a strangely calming effect. But the 'lodge' is no country bumpkin; the Tighes' renowned professionalism and standards of excellence are everywhere. Every room has the gorgeous view. Bedrooms are sophisticated and Moira Tighe's thoughtful touch much in evidence. The hairdrier is where it should be: on the dressing table. There are flowers and fruit; fresh milk for tea; chairs enticingly placed by the picture windows; every toilet requisite imaginable in the gleaming bathrooms. In the evenings, beds are turned down and curtains drawn. Christy knows about walks, archaeological sites and Yeats Country; Moira presides over her all-female classy kitchen. A special place, worth a special journey.

~

NEARBY Yeats Country; Lissadell House; Carrowkeel Cairns; Sligo.
LOCATION in own farmland, near village of Ballindoon; parking available
MEALS breakfast, dinner
PRICES rooms I£60-I£90pp; breakfast included; dinner I£25-I£38
ROOMS 10; all double/twin; all with bath and shower; all rooms with phone, tv, minibar, hairdrier, safe
FACILITIES sitting-room, bar; garden, terrace; fishing; helipad
CREDIT CARDS AE, DC, MC, V
CHILDREN welcome; cot; private family dining-room
DISABLED not possible
PETS not accepted
CLOSED Nov/Dec/Jan **PROPRIETORS** Christy and Moira Tighe

Co Galway

Clifden

The Ardagh Hotel

~ COAST HOTEL AND RESTAURANT ~

Ballyconneely Road, Clifden, Co Galway
Tel 095 21384 **Fax** 095 21314
E-MAIL ardaghhotel@tinet.ie

THIS IS SO CLOSE TO THE SEA you feel you could reach out and dip your toe in the water. The view from the restaurant over Ardbear Bay is fabulous: light and colours constantly change; sunsets are memorable. This small family hotel has a continental flavour that gives it considerable charm. Monique Bauvet's Dutch father bought the site and blasted a hole out of the limestone hillside for the blue and yellow, gabled, chalet-style building. She's the chef, housekeeper and gardener; her seafood chowder is a treat; her rooms are pristine (she's phasing out the flowery look for something more bright and contemporary); she made the garden among the rocks. Her husband, Stephane, can be found behind the front desk, or serving wine, and is always ready to help. They met in Switzerland and their hotel has a satisfying combination of friendliness and reliable, discreet efficiency. Locals frequent the downstairs bar lounge; Billie Holliday plays in the dining-room; the son of the house plays football in the car park with the receptionist. Not all the well-equipped rooms have sea views; ask when booking. Tucked under the eaves, a sunny sitting-room for residents has piles of magazines and a profusion of greenery. (In high season the coast road in front of the hotel could be busy.)

~

NEARBY Kylemore Abbey; Connemara National Park.
LOCATION on coast road S of Clifden; parking available
MEALS breakfast, bar lunch, dinner
PRICES rooms I£45-I£55pp; standard double I£100; breakfast included; lunch I£5; dinner I£26
ROOMS 21; 16 double/twin, 3 suites, 2 family; 19 with bath, 4 with shower only; all rooms with phone, tv, radio, hairdrier; tea/coffee making facilities; safe at reception
FACILITIES garden, terrace; bar lounge, restaurant, sun room
CREDIT CARDS AE, DC, MC, V
CHILDREN welcome **DISABLED** not possible **PETS** accepted
CLOSED Nov to Easter or Apr 1 **PROPRIETORS** Monique and Stephane Bauvet

Co Galway

CLIFDEN

MALLMORE HOUSE
~ COUNTRY BED-AND-BREAKFAST ~

Ballyconneely Road, Clifden, Co Galway
TEL 095 21460

THE HARDMANS BREED CONNEMARA PONIES, for showing and dressage; these hardy little natives are often kept beside the drive to the family's lovingly restored house with a cheery red front door and late Georgian porch. The place is stiff with historical interest: Baden Powell, founder of the Boy Scouts, used to spend his holidays here. Alan and Kathleen Hardman came from The New Inn at Tresco on the Isles of Scilly to work for themselves and found the house in a derelict state: only one room had been used since the 1920s. From the back of the house there is a lovely view through trees over the bay to Clifden and out to the Atlantic. You can walk down to the sea through the orchard and past the old cottage. Rooms in this unusual and intriguing, mainly single-storey house, with original pitch pine floors, have a variety of views; for water ask for Room 4. One room has the original washbasin, and wallpaper with a pattern of birds; another original wide shutters, yellow paper, a Bonnard print and spotless bathroom. Award-winning breakfasts are served in the dining-room, which also has its original shutters; tables have pink cloths. On the menu: smoked salmon pancakes; smoked mackerel; Irish bacon. Very much a family affair; a daughter bakes brown bread each evening.

~

NEARBY Clifden; Connemara National Park; Kylemore Abbey.
LOCATION a mile out of Clifden town centre; in own 35-acre grounds on Ardbear peninsula; parking available
MEALS breakfast
PRICES rooms I£18-I£20pp; standard double I£36-I£40; breakfast included
ROOMS 6; 3 double, 1 twin, 1 family room with 1 double and 2 singles, 1 with1 double and 1 single; all with showers and spring water; hairdriers in most rooms
FACILITIES gardens and woodland
CREDIT CARDS not accepted
CHILDREN welcome; 20% discount
DISABLED possible **PETS** not permitted in rooms **CLOSED** 1 Nov to 1 Mar
PROPRIETORS Alan and Kathleen Hardman

CO GALWAY

THE QUAY HOUSE
~ TOWNHOUSE ~

Beach Road, Clifden, Co Galway
TEL 095 21369 **FAX** 095 21608
E-MAIL thequay@iol.ie

PADDY FOYLE IS A CELEBRATED mover and shaker in this rapidly getting very hip little seaside town, where he was born in room 12 of Foyle's Hotel. He has a little blue-and-white restaurant called Destry's in Main Street and stylish Quay House, down on the harbour wall where the fishing boats tie up. A natural interior decorator, he has the boldness and panache of a set designer: the house, built in 1820 for the harbourmaster, is a stage for his fanciful ideas and outbursts of colour. You have the distinct sense you are in a production of some kind – is it an opera? a film? – as you pass through the wondrous rooms. A favourite theme is Scandinavian: washed-out, distressed paintwork; plenty of grey and Nordic blue; wooden panelling; striped fabrics. One room is a riot of blue *toile de Jouy*; there's a Napoleon Room at the top of the house; another has a frieze of scallop shells. It's pretty; it's fun. But Paddy is a restless pacer, always moving on, so expect changes. He's already stuck a bay on to the old flat-fronted house, bought the place next door and turned it into studios. On our visit, he had his eye on the conservatory, which was doing very nicely as a breakfast-room, where you may start the day with fresh white table cloths and china among the green plants. For now.

~

NEARBY Connemara National Park; Galway, 50 miles (80 km).
LOCATION on quay, 3 minutes by car from Clifden town centre; parking in road
MEALS breakfast
PRICES rooms I£35-I£45pp; standard double I£80; breakfast included
ROOMS 14; 5 superkings, 9 double (4 twin); all with bath and shower; all rooms with phone, tv, radio, hairdrier; 6 with balcony
FACILITIES sitting-room; garden, terrace
CREDIT CARDS AE, MC, V
CHILDREN welcome
DISABLED ground-floor rooms
PETS not accepted
CLOSED mid-Nov to mid-Mar **PROPRIETORS** Paddy and Julia Foyle

,CO GALWAY

ROCK GLEN COUNTRY HOUSE HOTEL

~ COUNTRY HOTEL ~

Clifden, Co Galway
TEL 095 21035 **FAX** 095 21737
E-MAIL rockglen@iol.ie

WITH CLEMATIS AND VIRGINIA CREEPER around the front door, Rock Glen is a proud winner of an award for the Most Romantic Hotel in Ireland and what we found was full of charm. The setting of this former shooting lodge, built in 1815, is glorious: in front of the hotel, a path through a meadow of long grass, wild flowers and yellow iris, leads to the shoreline. A yacht bobs about at anchor in the little bay. In the evenings, Connemara ponies and cattle come down to the water's edge. Rising up behind the hotel are the Twelve Pins mountains. With miles of sandy beaches nearby and rugged countryside criss-crossed with drystone walls, it's a lovely place to walk, or simply to sit and quietly enjoy watching the ebb and flow of the tide. Hosts John and Evangeline Roche (who was born in Clifden) are veterans who have thought of everything: a glassed-in extension to the bar has sofas in which to install yourself comfortably for the long view; turf fires; soft candlelight in the dining-room. They have taken the unusual step of reducing the number of bedrooms, to improve space and comfort for guests. Some rooms have balconies. The Roches' daughter, Siobhan, has come home to take over the management of this inviting, cosy place.

~

NEARBY Clifden; Connemara National Park; Kylemore Abbey.
LOCATION in own grounds by the sea, 1.5 miles S of Clifden on the N59 to Galway; parking available
MEALS breakfast, bar lunch, dinner
PRICES from I£65.25pp; standard double I£130.50; breakfast included; dinner I£31.50
ROOMS 26; 23 double/twin, 3 family rooms; all with bath/shower; all rooms have phone, tv, radio, hairdrier; trouser press
FACILITIES snooker table; putting green, croquet lawn, tennis court; tv room
CREDIT CARDS AE, DC, MC, V
DISABLED ground-floor rooms
PETS not in rooms
CLOSED mid-Jan to mid-Mar **PROPRIETORS** John and Evangeline Roche

Co Clare

COROFIN

CLIFDEN HOUSE
~ COUNTRY HOUSE ~

Corofin, Co Clare
TEL/FAX 065 6837692

One of the Hidden Ireland 'heritage' houses taking guests, this is listed, early Georgian, and stands on the wooded shore of Lake Inchiquin. When the Robsons found it, it had been abandoned for about 30 years: trees grew out of the roof; there were cows in the basement. Little by little, and most lovingly, they have brought it back to life. Guests will feel quite close to the work in hand, as in several places there are exposed bits of the innards of the lathe and plaster walls. There's quite a bit that Jim Robson hasn't got round to yet. It's a mammoth task, but herein lies the stuff of many of his amusing and entertaining stories. Ask Jim (who in his previous existence sold books in Hay-on-Wye) about the crooked mirrors. He is also something of an expert on the limestone Burren. When we visited, he was working on a new breakfast-room and a fern garden in a corner of dappled shade by the ruined mill and the little bridge over the River Fergus. Entered through handsome Georgian doorways, the smart bedrooms have virtually been hand-made by him. Colours are bold: green; yellow; red; blue. One has an old roll-top bath actually *in* the room. There's a tree house, a boat on the lake, an old walled kitchen garden. Prepare for a bit of an adventure, with good food, too.

~

NEARBY The Burren National Park; Ennis, 9 miles (14 km); Shannon, 26 miles (42 km).
LOCATION in lakeside grounds and woodland, 1 mile from Corofin; parking available
MEALS breakfast; dinner
PRICES rooms I£35pp; standard double I£70; dinner I£20
ROOMS 4; 3 double, 1 twin; 3 with bath, 1 with shower; all have hairdrier and books
FACILITIES garden; boat, bicycles, fishing rods
CREDIT CARDS AE, DC, MC, V
CHILDREN welcome **DISABLED** no facilities **PETS** not accepted
CLOSED mid-Dec to mid-Mar **PROPRIETORS** Jim and Bernadette Robson

Co Galway

KILLEEN HOUSE
~ GUEST-HOUSE ~

Killeen, Bushypark, Galway, Co Galway
TEL 091 524179 **FAX** 091 528065

WHAT ORIGINALITY AND IMAGINATION Catherine Doyle has shown in creating such charming quarters for guests in her fascinating early Victorian house. While the approach is somewhat dispiriting, through the outer suburbs of Galway and past new housing developments, once you get beyond the castellated gateway into the 25-acre garden and grounds, all that is forgotten in a trice. The interiors, packed with unusual antiques and bric-a-brac, are a feast for the eyes. The idea behind the bedrooms, Catherine explains, was 'to give everyone something different'. So, she has taken historical periods as themes: Regency; Victorian; Edwardian; Art Nouveau. But these are not artificial pastiches: they are comfortable, welcoming rooms that reflect the care Catherine puts into every aspect of running the house. (She writes the breakfast menu out by hand.) The detail goes right down to the sheets and hand towels. Each room has a reproduction radio, to fit in with the general style; each room even has its own pair of 'period' binoculars, for looking at birds when you take the path leading through the garden, past an old cottage, down to the shores of Lough Corrib. There is also the new Garden Suite; modern, for a change, with bright blue and yellow carpet and painted chairs.

NEARBY Galway city centre, 4 miles (6 km); Connemara; the Burren.
LOCATION in garden and grounds, 4 miles (6 km) from centre of Galway; parking available
MEALS breakfast
PRICES rooms I£35-I£45pp; standard double I£70-I£90; breakfast included
ROOMS 5; 4 double/1 twin; 4 with bath; 1 with shower; all with phone, tv, radio, hairdrier, tea/coffee making facilities
FACILITIES garden; drawing-room, dining-room
CREDIT CARDS AE, DC, MC, V
CHILDREN not suitable for children under 12
DISABLED not suitable **PETS** kennel for dogs
CLOSED Christmas **PROPRIETOR** Catherine Doyle

Co Galway

NORMAN VILLA
~ TOWNHOUSE ~

86 Lower Salthill, Galway, Co Galway
TEL/FAX 091 521131

Dee KEOGH THINKS that the term 'bed-and-breakfast' has had its day, conjuring up, as it does, images of an impersonal place where you arrive, are given a bed, some breakfast, and leave, with 'no chat, no conversation, no cups of tea'. How very unlike Norman Villa, tall, of grey stone, mid-19thC; a little haven of friendliness and appreciation of the good things in life. The entire house is beautiful: the black and white tiled floor in the hall; gleaming brass beds; varnished wood floors; original shutters, pine furniture. Always buyers of pictures, the Keoghs' collection of modern art hangs on the walls, along with prints of classical remains. There's something pleasing everywhere. A balloon-back chair. A combination of colours. Or Dee's brilliant showers disguised as cupboards. Her husband, Mark, cooks breakfast, served in the old kitchen, with its slate floor and yellow walls. These two have reached a kind of perfection; it is as much a pleasure watching them at work as enjoying their house. Dee dispenses tea, plenty of chat, and her home-made Porter cake; Mark, a former gunnery captain, gives helpful directions with military precision. Thoughtfully, they have printed little maps for guests; the best shows you how to get back to Norman Villa.

~

NEARBY city centre; the Burren; Connemara; Yeats' Tower; Coole Park.
LOCATION 15 minutes walk from city centre; parking available
MEALS breakfast
PRICES rooms I£32.50; standard double I£65; breakfast included
ROOMS 5; 4 double, 1 family with 2 double and 1 pull-out bed; all with shower; all with hairdrier
FACILITIES garden; sitting-room, dining-room
CREDIT CARDS MC, V
CHILDREN welcome
DISABLED not possible
PETS no dogs
CLOSED never **PROPRIETORS** Dee and Mark Keogh

Co Galway

KYLEMORE HOUSE
~ GUEST-HOUSE ~

Kylemore, Co Galway
TEL/FAX 095 41143

ONCE THE HOME of the poet Oliver St John Gogarty – who features in James Joyce's *Ulysses* – there's still a strong artistic flavour about this white house on the edge of Kylemore Lough, built for Lord Ardilaun in 1785. Owner Nancy Naughton says her regulars – mostly fishermen – don't want any changes; so the somewhat off-beat charm of the house seems to be unchanging. Something of a character herself, she has a strong aversion to TV in bedrooms: "What will they be wanting with television?" she asks. Quite so: the pictures alone would keep anyone engrossed for hours. She has a portrait of Queen Henrietta Maria, said to be school of Vandyke (maybe he did the face himself?), some fine sporting prints and many more. In St John Gogarty's former library, with its unusual ceiling, is a suite of French painted furniture she bought in an auction in England. She says her fishermen don't care much where they sleep, but the bedrooms are spacious and filled with interesting pieces. Downstairs rooms have welcoming peat fires in beautiful fireplaces. The kitchen is always busy: breakfast includes black and white pudding, and Mrs Naughton's home-made marmalade and brown bread; packed lunches; fishermen's teas; dinner is often, not surprisingly, salmon.

~

NEARBY Kylemore Abbey; Connemara National Park; Clifden.
LOCATION in garden and grounds, on the N59 to Clifden; parking available
MEALS breakfast, packed lunches, dinner
PRICES rooms I£18.50pp; standard double I£37; breakfast included; dinner I£17
ROOMS 7; 4 double, 2 twin, 1 single, 2 with bath, 5 with shower; hairdrier on request
FACILITIES garden; 3 private fishing lakes; sitting-rooms
CREDIT CARDS not accepted
CHILDREN not accepted
DISABLED 1 downstairs room
PETS dogs sleep in car
CLOSED Oct to Easter **PROPRIETOR** Mrs Nancy Naughton

CO GALWAY

DELPHI LODGE
~ FISHING LODGE ~

Leenane, Co Galway
TEL 095 42222 **FAX** 095 42296
E-MAIL delfish@iol.ie

THE 2ND MARQUESS OF SLIGO – who had been with Byron in Greece – thought this wild place as beautiful as Delphi, and built himself a fishing lodge here in the mid-1830s. When Peter Mantle, a former financial journalist, came across the house, it was semi-derelict. Falling under the same spell, he restored it with great care and vision, and Delphi is one of the finest and foremost sporting lodges in Ireland. Fishing is its main business, but everyone is made welcome here. Peter, a lively host and raconteur, runs it like a friendly country house. On our visit, on a misty April evening, wood smoke was rising from the chimney, a new delivery of Crozes Hermitage was stacked up in the hall and Mozart was playing in the snug little library overlooking the lake. Among the guests were a couple of bankers in their Jeremy Fisher waterproofs, a novelist finishing a book, and some Americans from Philadelphia. Salmon are weighed and measured in the Rod Room, creating frissons of excitement and stories for the communal dinner table; the ghillies come in during breakfast to discuss prospects for the day ahead. Bedrooms are unfussy but pretty, with pine furniture; larger ones have lake views; bathrooms have piles of fluffy, white towels. Book well ahead. Heaven for walkers.

~

NEARBY Westport, 20 miles (32 km); Kylemore Abbey; Clifden; golf.
LOCATION by the lake in wooded grounds on private estate; parking available
MEALS breakfast, lunch, dinner
PRICES rooms I£30pp-I£60pp; standard double with lake view I£90-I£120; other I£60-I£90; breakfast included; packed/light lunch I£8; dinner I£29
ROOMS 12; 5 standard, 7 with lake view; all double (4 twin); all with bath; all with phone; hairdrier available
FACILITIES gardens; lake; drawing-room, billiard room, library, data transmission
CREDIT CARDS AE, MC, V
CHILDREN welcome
DISABLED 2 ground-floor rooms **PETS** not permitted in house
CLOSED mid-Dec to mid-Jan **PROPRIETORS** Peter and Jane Mantle

Co Galway

KILLARY LODGE
~ COUNTRY ACCOMMODATION ~

Leenane, Co Galway
TEL 095 42276/42245/42302 **FAX** 095 42314
E-MAIL killary@iol.ie

A LONG, ROUGH TRACK through rhododendrons leads to this remote, former 19thC hunting and fishing lodge on the edge of Killary Harbour and looking towards Mweelrea, the great 'grey, bald mountain', the highest in Connacht. Aptly, what began life as a gentleman's sporting residence is now an activities centre run by Jamie Young, voyager and adventurer – who has followed in the steps of Shackleton, the Irish Atlantic explorer – and his wife, Mary. Here, you might well wake up to find that, during the night, some trans-Atlantic yachtsmen have arrived and moored at the jetty on the deep, tidal inlet. You can also spot sea otters, seals and dolphin. Everything is simple, basic and practical, with the home fires kept burning for guests who have been out cycling, walking, fishing, water-skiing, boating. There are plenty of drying facilities and a Drip Room. It's not all outward bound; you can curl up with a book if you don't wish to be energetic. Rooms – in the house or the converted stabling and cottage – are comfortable and well-equipped. Laundry can be done for you. There is no TV; the Youngs consider it a conversation-killer. The young, enthusiastic staff are much involved in the social side of things, that's the spirit of this friendly place.

~

NEARBY Leenane; Letterfrack; Clifden; Westport.
LOCATION in own grounds; 4 miles (6 km) from Leenane; parking available
MEALS breakfast, lunch, dinner
PRICES rooms I£29-I£37pp; standard double I£74; breakfast included; lunch from I£4.50; dinner I£20
ROOMS 21; 2 double, 5 twin, 2 with 3 beds, 7 family, 5 single, 9 with bath, 12 shower only; all rooms with phone; hairdrier on request; safe at reception
FACILITIES gardens; tennis; table-tennis; sauna; beach
CREDIT CARDS MC, V
CHILDREN welcome
DISABLED 3 ground-floor rooms **PETS** dogs in cars only; take care with sheep
CLOSED between Christmas and 17 Mar **PROPRIETORS** Jamie and Mary Young

CO CLARE

LISDOONVARNA

BALLINALACKEN CASTLE HOTEL
~ COUNTRY HOTEL ~

Lisdoonvarna, Co Clare
TEL/FAX 065 7074025

THIS FASCINATING HOUSE, high on a green hillside with uninterrupted Atlantic views, was built as a 'villa' in the 1840s for John O'Brien, MP for Limerick. Not only does it have its own ruins of a 15thC O'Brien stronghold, but the entrance hall with cupola and green Connemara marble fireplace remains more or less unaltered. There is a newish, discreetish extension, but main house bedrooms have large, dark, old-fashioned pieces of antique furniture, huge wardrobes, and original shutters. From the bed in Room 4, you can see the Aran islands; and Room 7 has a view of the Cliffs of Moher. The lay-out is intriguing – mostly on one floor. The air of faded grandeur is enlivened by the youthful enthusiasm of Marian O'Callaghan – her grandfather bought the castle ruins 50 years ago – and her husband, Frankie Sheedy, a chef of the 'Modern Irish' school. He puts Connemara lamb with courgettes, tomatoes and polenta, and local seafood with saffron cream. The dining-room has another cracker of a fireplace, turf fire, original wood floor, pink tablecloths. Nightcaps are served in the lounge bar, and you can steep yourself in the history of the place with locals and join in sing-alongs on weekend evenings, when live entertainment is laid on.

~

NEARBY The Burren; Ballyvaughan; Doolin Crafts Gallery
LOCATION in 100-acre grounds, 3 miles (5 km) S of Lisdoonvarna on R477; parking available
MEALS breakfast, bar lunch, dinner
PRICES rooms I£35-I£38pp; standard double I£70-I£76; breakfast included; lunch from I£5; dinner I£22
ROOMS 13; 2 king-size double, 4 standard double, 7 with double and single bed; 10 with bath, all with shower; all with phone, tv, radio, hairdrier
FACILITIES garden; sitting-room, bar
CREDIT CARDS MC, V **CHILDREN** welcome **DISABLED** not suitable
PETS well-behaved dogs in room; not in public areas **CLOSED** mid-Oct to mid-Apr
PROPRIETORS Denis and Mary O'Callaghan

Co Clare

LISDOONVARNA

SHEEDY'S RESTAURANT AND HOTEL
~ RESTAURANT WITH ROOMS ~

Lisdoonvarna, Co Clare
TEL 065 7074026 **FAX** 065 7074555
E-MAIL cmv@indigo.ie

THIS SMALL HOTEL was originally a farmhouse where the Sheedy family began looking after visitors to this little spa town (it has sulphurous springs) in 1855. Recently, however, some bright, new changes have taken place: John Sheedy, ex-Ashford Castle head chef, has come home to cook; his delightful wife, Martina, looks after front of house and the wine list; and adds her taste for contemporary design. John Sheedy's food is highly acclaimed and the restaurant has been given a completely new look to complement his celebrated 'Modern Irish' cooking. Walls are painted in a moody grey colour called 'Muddy River'. Martina, who used to work at Mount Juliet, has also begun her transformation of the hotel, bringing in help from the nearby Doolin Craft Gallery, renowned for sharp, simple design in wool, crystal, linen and tweed. The lobby already heralds the exciting shape of things to come, with shiny wood floor, little curved reception desk, a bit of exposed natural stone, paintwork in gentian blue and terracotta red. She can't wait to get upstairs, where bedrooms are to be upgraded; the priority is to be comfort, she says, but some modern design "will be in there somewhere". A place to watch; reports, please.

~

NEARBY The Burren; Ballyvaughan; Doolin Craft Gallery.
LOCATION in centre of Lisdoonvarna, on edge of the Burren; parking available
MEALS breakfast, lunch, dinner
PRICES rooms I£25-I£32.50pp; standard double I£65; breakfast included; seafood bar lunch from I£10; dinner I£25 (early evening I£15.95)
ROOMS 11; 5 double, 6 twin; 9 with bath, 2 with shower; all with phone, tv, hairdrier; ironing board available
FACILITIES south-facing sun lounge, seafood bar, sitting-room, restaurant
CREDIT CARDS AE, MC, V
CHILDREN welcome **DISABLED** not possible
PETS not accepted
CLOSED end Sept to Easter
PROPRIETORS the Sheedy family

CO GALWAY

MOYARD

CROCNARAW
~ COUNTRY GUEST-HOUSE ~

Moyard, Co Galway
TEL 095 41068

WE WERE SOMEWHAT unsure about promoting Crocnaraw to a full page in 1997's expanded edition. Either you will love it, or you will wish you had gone elsewhere. One of our most experienced reporters thought it was wonderful, despite some obvious areas of disrepair – or perhaps because of them. She felt that the place had a great deal of the special quality we look for. At the same time, we have also received letters from readers who are severely critical of the housekeeping, and who consider Crocnaraw to be poor value for money.

Crocnaraw is certainly the antithesis of the glossy hotel: white is the dominant colour theme, but it is very imaginatively decorated with local 'tweed, rugs, cushions and so on, in gentle colours, with some antique pieces and some modern pieces, wooden and slate floors'. The long, low Georgian building is set on a small hill-top in lush, prize-winning gardens.

The food is 'definitely above average for an Irish hotel', 'imaginative without being fussy'; proper attention is given to breakfast. Lucy Fretwell makes a 'vague but charming hostess'. Come here if you want a 'special atmosphere and a truly peaceful, wonderfully relaxed retreat'. If you want something more conventional in this area, see Rosleague Manor (page 138). Reports welcome.

~

NEARBY Kylemore Abbey, 5 miles (8 km); Kylemore Abbey, 5 miles (8 km); Joyce Country.
LOCATION 6 miles (10 km) N of Clifden, on shores of Ballinakill Bay; in 20-acre grounds, with ample parking **MEALS** full breakfast, lunch, dinner; full licence
PRICES B&B I£25-I£45; dinner I£20; reduced DB&B rates for 3 or 7 nights
ROOMS 8; 6 double with bath, one also with shower; 2 single; all rooms have central heating **FACILITIES** 2 sitting-rooms, dining-room; fishing, riding and golf nearby **CREDIT CARDS** AE, DC, MC, V **CHILDREN** accepted by arrangement
DISABLED access easy to one ground-floor bedroom **PETS** dogs welcome except in dining-room **CLOSED** Nov to Apr **PROPRIETOR** Lucy Fretwell

Co Mayo

MULRANNY

ROSTURK WOODS

~ COUNTRY GUEST-HOUSE ~

Rosturk, Mulranny, Co Mayo
TEL/FAX 098 36264
E-MAIL stoney@iol.ie

IT IS NO SURPRISE that word of Alan and Louisa Stoney's charming little complex among trees on the tidal, sandy shore of Clew Bay has spread so far. First of all it's a paradise for children – with the doorstep on the beach, so to speak. When the tide is out, you can walk across to an island and there is plenty to see in the way of wildlife. The Stoneys' adaptable newly-built family house was completed in 1991; an even newer self-catering cottage opened for business in 1999 and was booked – immediately – for the summer. But the buildings blend nicely into the leafy background, and with wood fires, wooden floors and lots of painted furniture, the house has a open, airy, seaside feel about it, which is instantly relaxing. Rooms are comfortable; some are up under the eaves. Louisa is a reflexologist when she is not looking after guests. Her ops centre is her enormous kitchen, with dogs, pots and pans, children's paintings on the wall, and windows facing south to the water. From here comes the freshly squeezed orange juice and smoked salmon and scrambled egg for breakfast; dinner could be organic spinach soup, fresh black sole from Achill Island (the fish man delivers daily), and home-made ice cream. The house has two boats; Alan is a sailing instructor.

NEARBY Westport, 18 miles (29 km); Achill Island, 11 miles (18 km); Newport, 7 miles (11 km).
LOCATION 3 miles before Mulranny on the Newport/Achill road; in 5-acre grounds with parking
MEALS breakfast, dinner
PRICES rooms I£25-I£30pp; standard double I£50-I£60; 3 with sea view; breakfast included; dinner I£20
ROOMS 4; 2 double, 2 twin; 2 with bath and shower, 2 with shower; radio on request; all with hairdrier
FACILITIES tennis court; snooker room; garden; woodland; beach
CREDIT CARDS not accepted **CHILDREN** welcome **DISABLED** not possible
PETS welcome **CLOSED** 1 Dec to 1 Mar **PROPRIETORS** Alan and Louisa Stoney

Co Tipperary

NENAGH

ASHLEY PARK HOUSE

~ COUNTRY HOUSE BED-AND-BREAKFAST ~

Ardcrony, Nenagh, Co Tipperary
TEL/FAX 067 38223

A PEACOCK WAS SITTING, wailing, on the rail of the green veranda when we visited Ashley Park: one of the owner's beloved birds that are fed every morning in a ritual of the household. Mr Mounsey, who has a grocery store in Nenagh, is insistent that nothing here should be like a hotel. He need have no fears on that front. This wildly atmospheric early 18thC house comes complete with ballroom, ruined chapel on an island on the lake, original stabling and farmyard in a more-or-less untouched state, and a scheduled Neolithic ring fort in the woods. The whole place is a nature reserve, too. Mr Mounsey likes every guest to be given an electric blanket; Mozart is played at breakfast and Frank Sinatra at dinner. We were unable to see any bedrooms, as they were occupied by a sleeping film crew, but, like all the other rooms in the house, they are huge, as are the bathrooms with their Victorian fittings. The Irish President, Mary McAleese, has stayed in Room 2. Roses trail along the veranda that runs the length of the house and, to relax, you can sit and read in the octagonal Chinese Room. There are turf fires; Mr Mounsey's daughter, Margaret, bakes a delicious scone; fresh eggs can be ordered straight from the hen. Hotels just don't come like this.

~

NEARBY Lough Derg; Limerick, 27 miles (43 km); Shannon.
LOCATION on private estate, with lake, 3.5 miles (6 km) out of Nenagh on Borrisokane road; parking available
MEALS breakfast; dinner
PRICES rooms I£20pp sharing; I£23 single; standard double I£40; breakfast included; dinner I£18
ROOMS 6; 3 double, 2 twin, 1 family; 3 with bath and shower, 3 with shower; tv and hairdrier on request
FACILITIES garden; lake, boat, fishing rods, riding; public telephone
CREDIT CARDS not accepted
CHILDREN welcome
DISABLED not possible **PETS** accepted **CLOSED** never **PROPRIETOR** Sean Mounsey

CO CLARE

NEWMARKET-ON-FERGUS

CARRYGERRY COUNTRY HOUSE
~ COUNTRY HOUSE HOTEL ~

Newmarket-on-Fergus, Co Clare
TEL 061 363739 **FAX** 061 363823
E-MAIL carrygerryhotel@hotmail.com

BEING SO CONVENIENTLY close to Shannon airport – a ten-minute drive away – this could have settled for being a commercial hotel. But the kindness and warm hospitality of Marinus van Kooyk and his wife, Angela, have made this old manor house into a place to remember for those staying for either their first or last night in Ireland. In gardens, woodland, and pasture – now home to two donkeys – Carrygerry, built in the 18thC with a gable end and a remarkable courtyard entered through an archway, was a private house until as recently as the 1980s. Angela is passionate about her house and she has filled it with antiques and pretty things. The two cosy sitting-rooms, either side of the front door, are delightful places to pass away the time, with blazing fires, deep sofas, striped cushions, oriental carpets, and rich, dark colours. The house really seems to come alive in the evenings, when it positively glows in candlelight. Mr van Kooyk used to work for an international hotel group, so standards are high. Daughter Elena, who works at Shannon, brings news from the airport. In the former coach house in the courtyard is a bar; some bedrooms are there, too. At the end of a flight or a long drive, this is a comfortable, welcoming traveller's rest.

~

NEARBY Shannon airport, 8 miles (13 km); Limerick, 20 miles (32 km); Ennis (32 km).
LOCATION in gardens and grounds; parking available
MEALS breakfast, lunch, dinner
PRICES rooms I£39-I£49pp; standard doubleI£98; breakfast included; lunch I£12-I£17; dinner I£25
ROOMS 12; 7 double, 3 twin, 2 single; 6 in courtyard; 10 with bath, 2 with shower; all with phone, tv, radio; hairdrier on request
FACILITIES grounds; courtyard; bar
CREDIT CARDS AE, DC, MC, V
CHILDREN over-12s welcome **DISABLED** possible **PETS** accepted **CLOSED** 3/4 Mar to 10/15 Mar **PROPRIETORS** Marinus and Angela van Kooyk

CO TIPERRARY

PUCKANE

ST DAVID'S COUNTRY HOUSE AND RESTAURANT

~ COUNTRY HOUSE HOTEL ~

Puckane, Nenagh, Co Tipperary
TEL 067 24145 **FAX** 067 24388

ST DAVID'S WAS ORIGINALLY a fishing lodge built in 1798 for a Protestant clergyman and then rebuilt in stone in Victorian times. It is not so much on the edge of Lough Derg, but so close that, in some lights, it looks as if the waters of the lake might well spill over the harbour wall where the swans dally. The interiors are charming and decorated with great originality: the breakfast-room has blue-and-white striped wallpaper and a row of children's shoes on a shelf; a bedroom has curtains covered with swathes of blue ribbons; there's a pile of antique luggage under the stairs. Bathrooms are spotless, bedrooms are large and extremely comfortable. The pink and green Dublin Room has a four-poster bed and view of the lake. But the real point of this place is eating. Austrian Bernhard Klotz is chef and part-owner and most of the produce used in his classic French and Italian dishes comes from the home farm and garden. He spent two years searching for the perfect house to suit his purposes. His staff share his dedication. Our inspector found his assistant manager, Astrid, lovingly tying green ribbons around napkins in the dining room. In the evening, rabbits scoot over the neat lawns and on the other side of the lake are the twinkling lights of Dromineen.

~

NEARBY Nenagh Heritage Centre, 6 miles (10 km); Limerick, 45 miles (72 km).
LOCATION in lakeside gardens and grounds, 6 miles (10 km) from Nenagh; parking available
MEALS breakfast, dinner
PRICES rooms I£60-I£90pp; standard double I£120; breakfast included; dinner I£32
ROOMS 10; 8 double, 2 twin; 1 with bath, 9 with shower; all with phone, radio, hairdrier; dressing-gown
FACILITIES lakeside gardens, terrace; sitting-room, conservatory
CREDIT CARDS AE, MC, V **CHILDREN** welcome
DISABLED possible **PETS** not in bedrooms **CLOSED** 15 Jan to end of Mar/beg Apr
PROPRIETORS Bernhard Klotz and partners

Co Galway

Lough Inagh Lodge Hotel
~ Country hotel ~

Inagh Valley, Recess, Co Galway
Tel 095 34706 **Fax** 095 34708
e-mail inagh@iol.ie

THIS SOLID, WELL-PROPORTIONED Victorian shooting lodge, romantically placed on one of the most beautiful lakes in Connemara, was boarded up when Maire O'Connor and her late husband, John, came across it looking for somewhere suitable to run as a small hotel. Remarkably, some of the old sporting record books survive and may be read by guests. Little has been overlooked in the way of comfort. Each bedroom, named after an Irish writer, has a dressing-room with trouser press (not that we rate these very highly as creature comforts, but they're useful for damp Connemara days). Views are of water and The Twelve Bens mountains. Maire has kept to rich dark Victorian colours and polished wood; her careful attention to detail and service is reflected throughout the comfortable, cosy house. She arranges the fresh flowers, which are sent from Clifden. Rooms downstairs have inviting log fires and warm lighting. The green dining-room with yellow curtains and gleaming, dark wood floor is delightful. Seafood and traditional wild game dishes are specialities of the kitchen. Loughs Inagh and Derryclare are on the doorstep; for walkers, there are miles of tracks through the wild and rugged landscape. The hotel also has a stable of bicycles.

~

Nearby Recess; Oughterard; Clifden; Galway.
Location in open country on shores of Lough Inagh; parking available
Meals breakfast, lunch, dinner
Prices rooms I£68-I£79pp; standard double I£136; breakfast included; lunch I£5-I£15; dinner I£10-I£27.50
Rooms 12; 8 double; 4 twin; all with bath and shower; all rooms have phone, tv, radio, hairdrier, trouser press; ironing board on request
Facilities garden; lake, fishing, bicycles
Credit cards AE, DC, MC, V
Children welcome **Disabled** ground-floor room
Pets acccepted
Closed mid-Dec to mid-Mar **Proprietor** Maire O'Connor

Co Sligo

RIVERSTOWN

COOPERSHILL
~ COUNTRY HOUSE HOTEL ~

Riverstown, Co Sligo
TEL 071 65108 **FAX** 071 65466

BRIAN O'HARA HAS BEEN RUNNING this delightful country house with his wife, Lindy, for the past twelve years now, and has subtly improved the style of the place without interfering with its essential appeal.

It is a fine house – though some may not think it elegant by Georgian standards – with splendidly large rooms (including the bedrooms, most of which have four-poster or canopy beds). It is furnished virtually throughout with antiques; but remains emphatically a home, with no hotel-like formality – and there is the unusual bonus of a table-tennis room to keep children amused.

The grounds are extensive enough not only to afford complete seclusion, but also to accommodate a river on which there is boating and fishing for pike and trout.

Lindy cooks honest country dinners based on English and Irish dishes, which are entirely in harmony with the nature of the place, while Brian knowledgeably organizes the cellar.

~

NEARBY Sligo, l2 miles (20 km); Lough Arrow; Lough Gara.
LOCATION 1 mile (1.5 km) W of Riverstown, off N4 Dublin-Sligo road; in large garden on 500-acre estate, with ample car parking
MEALS full breakfast, light or packed lunch, dinner; restaurant licence
PRICES B&B I£50-I£67; dinner I£26; reductions for 3 or more nights; 75% reduction for children under 12 sharing with parents
ROOMS 9; 8 double, 6 with bath, one with separate bath, one with shower; 1 family room with bath; all rooms have tea/coffee kit
FACILITIES sitting-room, dining-room; boating, fishing, tennis
CREDIT CARDS AE, DC, MC, V
CHILDREN welcome if well behaved
DISABLED no access
PETS welcome if well behaved, but not allowed in public rooms or bedrooms
CLOSED Nov to end Mar
PROPRIETORS Brian and Lindy O'Hara

Co Limerick

ADARE

CLONUNION HOUSE
~ FARMHOUSE BED-AND-BREAKFAST ~

Croom Road, Adare, Co Limerick
TEL/FAX 061 396657

A EWE WITH TWIN LAMBS had squeezed under the gate of her field and was heading, with determination, for a rose bush when our inspector visited. This is a group of buildings that used to be the stud farm of the Earls of Dunraven of nearby Adare Manor (now a hotel). Now, the Fitzgeralds raise fallow deer in the stallion paddocks and keep Charolais cattle as well as sheep. So the view from the Georgian farmhouse is of creatures as far as the eye can see.(The bizarre edifice on one side is a water tower.) The stable yards are not quite as well-kept as they once were, and the headstones in the horses' cemetery among the trees behind the house are overgrown. But there are many plans for improvements. Mary Fitzgerald is a charming, helpful hostess who always has time to chat and is happy to take on extras such as ironing. The sitting- and dining-rooms are on the raised ground floor, with elegant, tall Georgian windows. Mary keeps a wood fire burning in the evenings for guests; she says visitors like to sit and talk or pick out one of her collection of books from the shelves rather than watch TV. Breakfast is served across the hall in the dining-room. From Mary's kitchen come Irish bacon and eggs, pancakes, scones and freshly-baked bread. Bedrooms are spacious. For dinner, Adare, which has plenty of restaurants, is a short walk away.

~

NEARBY Adare; Limerick, 12 miles (19 km)
LOCATION among trees in gardens and grounds; parking available
MEALS breakfast; dinner by arrangement
PRICES rooms I£20pp; standard double I£40; breakfast included; dinner I£12
ROOMS 4; 1 double, 1 with 1 double and 2 single, 2 with a double and 1 single; 1 with bath, 3 with shower; all rooms with phone, hairdrier, tea/coffee making facilities
FACILITIES garden
CREDIT CARDS AE, MC, V **CHILDREN** welcome **DISABLED** not possible
PETS not in the house; care to be taken with stock **CLOSED** 1 Nov to 1 Apr
PROPRIETOR Mary Fitzgerald

CO KERRY

KILLEEN HOUSE HOTEL
~ COUNTRY HOTEL ~

Aghadoe, Lakes of Killarney, Co Kerry
TEL 064 31711 **FAX** 31811
E-MAIL charming@indigo.ie

WE HAD TO VISIT A HOTEL with 'charming' as its e-mail address. And there it was: a charming small hotel, a rectory built in 1838 and given a bright new white front and architectural twiddly bits painted in red by Michael and Geraldine Rosney, who took it over in 1992. Michael is a jolly, amusing - and kind - person who used to manage the Great Southern Hotel in Killarney. He has created not so much a quiet retreat from crowded Killarney (a I£5 taxi drive away), but a warm, cosy, entertaining and lively little place, where he spoils his golfing clients and indulges their every whim. He sees them off in the morning and waits for their return in the evening, like an anxious parent. Then he is to be found in The Pub, 'possibly the only place in the universe that accepts golf balls as legal tender', where he dispenses Guinness and sympathy. Nothing is too much trouble for him: he puts phone messages in envelopes and distributes them himself. All this activity provides loads of fun for everyone, especially Michael, and you don't have to be a golfer to benefit from his generous spirit. Comfortable, spacious bedrooms are often decorated in checks and plaids; he has got a special one with a spa bath that he gives to regular guests as a 'thank you' for coming back again and again. Good showers; excellent food.

~

NEARBY Killarney, 4 miles (6 km); Muckross House; Gap of Dunloe; lakes.
LOCATION in countryside, 4 miles (6 km) from Killarney; parking available
MEALS breakfast, dinner
PRICES rooms I£45-I£65pp; standard double I£90; breakfast included; dinner I£27.50
ROOMS 23; 8 championship, 15 standard; 8 with king-size double and single; 2 double, 5 twin, 2 single, 6 double and single; 22 with bath, 1 with shower; all with phone, tv, radio, hairdrier
FACILITIES garden, terrace, tennis court; bar, sitting-room **CREDIT CARDS** AE, DC, MC,V **CHILDREN** welcome if well-behaved **DISABLED** not possible **PETS** welcome
CLOSED 1 Nov to 1 Apr **PROPRIETORS** Michael and Geraldine Rosney

CO LIMERICK

BALLINGARRY

THE MUSTARD SEED AT ECHO LODGE

∼ COUNTRY HOUSE AND RESTAURANT ∼

Ballingarry, Co Limerick
TEL 069 68508 **FAX** 069 68511
E-MAIL mustard@bestloved.com

DAN MULLANE WON HIS SPURS with a restaurant in a tiny thatched cottage in Adare, often called the prettiest village in Ireland. Now he's moved his chefs to a shiny new kitchen in a former convent a few miles away, where he's blissfully happy gathering herbs in the vegetable garden and master of a much larger domaine. Echo Lodge is painted yellow, and has blue pots on the doorstep; he's filled the niches left empty when the nuns moved out with figures of Buddha, to whose calming powers he lights candles in the evenings. His regulars are as happy as he is. 'Foodies' flock to his blue-walled dining-room with the yellow laburnum outside the window. In season, you may well find a big dark pink peony on the table. Service is smooth, professional and busy. Mullane is very 'hands on'. It takes a brave man to keep the green baize door to the kitchen propped open: he does. Breakfast could be stewed prunes with an Earl Grey and lemon syrup, or porridge with cream and Irish whiskey. Among his many gifts, Dan can design a pretty bedroom, too. He likes French toiles, wallpaper striped like a Jermyn Street shirt, and fresh, gleaming white bathrooms; two of his most successful rooms are all in black and white. 'Is this paradise?' asks an Argentinian in the visitors' book.

∼

NEARBY Adare; Limerick, 18 miles (29 km); Shannon airport, 33 miles (53 km).
LOCATION in 7 acres of gardens and orchard on edge of village; parking available
MEALS breakfast, snack lunch, dinner
PRICES rooms I£60-I£80pp; standard double I£120; breakfast included; lunch I£3.50; dinner I£31
ROOMS 11; 8 double, 2 twin, 1 single; 7 with bath; 5 with shower; all with phone, tv, hairdrier; 8 with trouser press; safe at reception
FACILITIES gardens, terraces
CREDIT CARDS AE, MC, V
CHILDREN by arrangement
DISABLED possible
PETS by arrangement **CLOSED** Feb **PROPRIETOR** Dan Mullane

Co Cork

BALLYLICKEY MANOR HOUSE
~ COUNTRY HOUSE HOTEL ~

Ballylickey, Bantry Bay, Co Cork
TEL 027 50071 **FAX** 027 50124

THIS FORMER SHOOTING LODGE, with romantic view of the sea from the front door, is a *grande dame* of the Irish country house hotel scene – the first to be accepted by the Relais and Chateaux group in 1967. So it has all the requisite comfort and style – and some extra very French touches added by Christiane Graves' talent with colours, fabrics and antiques. As a private family house, it was visited many times by the writer and poet, Robert Graves, uncle of owner George Graves, whose mother, Kitty, laid out the lovely gardens. Some rooms are in the main house; one has doors opening on to a little sheltered patio with table and chairs for sitting out; or you may choose simply to let in the sound of birdsong and the wonderful damp smell of the plants and foliage. You are even closer to nature in the blue-grey wooden cottages in the trees and shrubs by the swimming-pool. With the sound of French staff chattering away in the kitchen of the poolside Le Rendez-Vous restaurant – covered in May with clouds of pink clematis – it is not hard to imagine oneself in a Relais and Chateaux in the South of France. Full marks should go to Mr Graves for his decision – possibly an unpopular one with some guests – not to allow parking in front of the house, which wrecks the sea view, by placing obstacles on the gravel driveway.

~

NEARBY Ring of Kerry; Killarney; Bantry.
LOCATION in gardens and grounds, on N17 between Bantry and Glengariff; parking available
MEALS breakfast, lunch, dinner
PRICES rooms I£65-I£90; standard double I£130; breakfast included; lunch I£15; dinner I£25
ROOMS 11; 7 suites, 4 double; all with bath and shower, phone, tv, hairdrier
FACILITIES swimming-pool; 3 sitting-rooms; garden, terraces; restaurant
CREDIT CARDS AE, DC, MC, V **CHILDREN** welcome
DISABLED poolside cottage **PETS** not accepted **CLOSED** end Oct to beg Apr
PROPRIETORS George and Christiane Graves

CO CORK

BALLYLICKEY

SEA VIEW HOUSE
~ COUNTRY HOTEL ~

Ballylickey, Bantry, Co Cork
TEL 027 50073 **FAX** 027 51555

KATHLEEN O'SULLIVAN GREW UP in this white Victorian house, a stone's throw from Ballylickey Bay. In 1978 she turned it into a successful small hotel. Her plan for an extension, to give double the number of rooms, was finally realized in 1990. 'Kathleen is a *delightful* hostess,' writes a recent reporter, and Sea View really is a 'very nice, quiet comfortable hotel'.

The new bedrooms are all similar in style, beautifully decorated in pastel colours and floral fabrics with stunning antique furniture – especially the bed-heads and wardrobes, and matching 3-piece suites, collected or inherited from around the Cork area. The rooms in the old part of the house are more irregular and individual. All front rooms have large bay windows and views of the garden and sea (through the trees). The 'Garden Suite' downstairs is especially adapted for wheelchairs.

There are two sitting-rooms – a cosy front room adjoining the bar and a large family room at the back. The dining-room has also been extended (though many regular guests do not believe it). Our reporter thought the food 'excellent and generous'; breakfast was 'wonderful' with a big choice and traditional Irish dishes, such as potato cakes. The menu changes daily, and Kathleen is forever experimenting with new dishes – roast smoked pheasant on the day we visited.

~

NEARBY Bantry, 3 miles (5 km); Beira Peninsula; Ring of Kerry.
LOCATION in countryside, just off N71, 3 miles (5 km) N of Bantry; in large grounds with ample car parking **MEALS** breakfast, lunch (Sun only), dinner; full licence
PRICES B&B I£40-I£55; dinner I£23.50; reductions for children sharing, and for stays of 3 or 7 days **ROOMS** 17; 14 double, 13 with bath, one with shower; 3 family rooms, all with bath; all rooms have central heating, phone, TV, hairdrier
FACILITIES 2 dining-rooms, sitting-room, TV room, bar **CREDIT CARDS** AE, MC, V
CHILDREN welcome; baby-sitting **DISABLED** access easy – one ground-floor adapted room **PETS** dogs accepted in bedrooms only
CLOSED Nov to Mar **PROPRIETOR** Kathleen O'Sullivan

CO CORK

BALTIMORE

THE ALGIERS INN

∼ VILLAGE INN ∼

Baltimore, Co Cork
TEL 028 20145 **FAX** 028 21675
E-MAIL jkwalsh@tinet.ie

THIS IS HARD TO BEAT on price or atmosphere. Baltimore, a fishing village and popular sailing centre, buzzes with life in the summer. Kieron Walsh has rooms which are basic and clean, up a little narrow staircase above his snug, traditional bar and restaurant His mother, Ellen, is housekeeper, and has more guest rooms next door at The Old Post House. She hangs the inn's sheets and towels out on the washing line in the garden and serves breakfast in her front room, which has hooks for hanging up sides of bacon, left over from the days when the post office sold anything from needles to boots. A steel pillar props up the ceiling; old gas lamps have been converted to electricity. Large windows – with spider plants cascading out of hanging baskets – look on to the street and the overgrown ruins of O'Driscoll's Castle opposite. Over a substantial Irish breakfast, including Clonakilty black and white pudding, Mrs Walsh can tell you about the infamous Sack of Baltimore in 1631, when Algerian pirates came into the harbour, killed two people, and took more than a hundred locals back to North Africa as slaves. On rough nights, you might find sailors coming in for a shower and a bed on dry land; Kieron serves a terrific plate of fresh haddock or whiting, more or less straight off the pier, with chips and salad.

∼

NEARBY Skibbereen; Mizen Head; Bantry; Cork.
LOCATION in village centre; street parking
MEALS breakfast, lunch in season, dinner
PRICES rooms I£16.50pp; single I£23; standard double I£33; breakfast included; lunch (June to Sept) I£5; dinner I£9.50
ROOMS 5 (7 next door); 2 double, 2 twin,1 family; all with wash-basin; shower across the corridor; hairdrier, iron on request
FACILITIES restaurant; sun terrace, beer garden
CREDIT CARDS MC, V **CHILDREN** welcome **DISABLED** not possible
PETS not in rooms; in kennels by arrangement **CLOSED** Christmas week
PROPRIETOR Kieron Walsh

Co Cork

BANTRY HOUSE

~ HERITAGE HOUSE WITH GUEST ACCOMMODATION ~

Bantry, Co Cork
TEL 027 50047 **FAX** 50795

IN A SPECTACULAR SETTING on a hillside overlooking Bantry Bay, this is one of the most beautiful houses in Ireland. It is filled with treasures brought home in the19thC by the 2nd Earl of Bantry from his European travels: a fireplace believed to have come from the Petit Trianon; a tapestry made for Marie Antoinette. He also set out a lovely formal Italian garden and a 'staircase to the sky', a flight of steps that, from the top, gives a view of the sea over the roof of the house. The current owner, Egerton Shelswell-White, was farming in Alabama when he inherited the house (it has belonged to his family since 1739) on his mother's death. It had been sadly neglected and there was a great deal of restoration work to be done. Guests stay in comfortable and snug quarters in a specially-adapted wing of the house; some rooms have sea views, others overlook the Italian garden and stone steps and terracing. Bedrooms have family furniture and bathrooms have lashings of hot water. You are given a key to the front door so you are free to walk in the gardens in the middle of the night and look at the stars over Bantry Bay. There's a billiards room with drinks tray and a little sitting-room with a fire. Mr Shelswell-White, a music-lover, waits at table and is a charming host. A tour of the house comes after breakfast.

~

NEARBY Bantry; Ring of Kerry; Killarney; Cork, 50 miles (80 km).
LOCATION in gardens and grounds overlooking Bantry Bay; main entrance in Bantry Town; with parking
MEALS breakfast, lunch (tea room), dinner
PRICES rooms I£65pp-I£75pp; standard double I£150; breakfast and house tour included; lunch I£5; dinner I£25
ROOMS 8; 6 in East Wing, 2 in West Wing; 5 double, 2 twin, 1 family; all with bath, shower, phone, hairdrier, tea/coffee making facilities
FACILITIES billiard room, tea room; gardens; shop; tennis **CREDIT CARDS** AE, MC, V
CHILDREN welcome **DISABLED** no downstairs rooms **PETS** not in rooms
CLOSED end Oct to early Mar **PROPRIETORS** Egerton and Brigitte Shelswell-White

Co Cork

BUTLERSTOWN HOUSE
∾ COUNTRY HOUSE ∾

Butlerstown, Bandon, Co Cork
TEL/FAX 023 40137
MOBILE 087 2203672

L IS JONES AND ROGER OWEN are an obviously happy couple who appear to
be over the moon with their escape from South Wales to the lovely
light and landscape of West Cork and the elegant spaces of this delightful
Georgian house. Their pleasure is infectious and gives the place a special
warmth. The airy rooms are filled with fine antiques – Roger is, usefully, a
furniture restorer as well as 'butler' – and classic colours enhance the
simple lines and architectural details of the house. A smart navy-blue
front door leads into the hall with bifurcated staircase; ornate plasterwork
in the house takes the shape of scallop shells, flowers, grapes, vine leaves
and ribbon tied into bows. Lis's bathrooms are a treat: she likes brass
taps, heated towel rails, blue-and-white striped tiles. There's a four-poster
in one room and twin French mahogany beds in another. The drawing-
room has a hi-fi and view of the bluebell wood where badgers roam at
night; the dining-room has a long, polished table and Spode on a
Monmouth dresser. Lis's breakfasts have a Celtic flavour with cockles and
laver bread; there's local milk, butter, and free-range eggs, as well as
smoked salmon and haddock. Some of the best things about living in
Butlerstown House, say Roger and Lis, are the fresh air and the stars in
the West Cork night sky.

∾

NEARBY Kinsale; Clonakilty; Bandon; Cork.
LOCATION in 10-acre gardens and grounds; parking available
MEALS breakfast, dinner on request for house parties only
PRICES rooms I£35-I£55pp; standard double I£90; breakfast and cream tea on
arrival included; dinner I£25
ROOMS 4; 2 double, 2 twin; 2 with bath, 2 with shower; all rooms with hairdrier,
electric blanket; tv on request
FACILITIES garden, terrace
CREDIT CARDS MC, V
CHILDREN over 12 **DISABLED** not possible **PETS** by arrangement
CLOSED Christmas to beg Feb

CO KERRY

CAMP

BARNAGH BRIDGE
~ COUNTRY GUEST-HOUSE ~

Camp, Tralee, Co Kerry
TEL 066 7130145 **FAX** 066 7130299

OVERLOOKING THE SANDY BEACHES of Tralee Bay on the north side of the Dingle Peninsula is this modern guest-house-with-a-difference. Some locals were bemused when it was first built, but now the landscaping is softening and the building appears to have settled comfortably into its background. What Heather Williams got when she asked her husband, Michael, to design a house where she could take in guests was inspired by his hero: Charles Rennie Mackintosh, the Scottish architect, artist and furniture maker. The spirit of the great man is very much here: plain, unadorned exterior; plenty of straight lines. Wings of the house have chimneys in the gables and fireplaces form focal points. An architect himself, he's used glass bricks for walls and to bring shafts of sunlight into the living areas; mirrors, jute carpeting, natural materials and fabrics enhance the impression of space and clarity. It's been a trifle difficult to 'design' out the view of a caravan site, but after a while, in this calm, orderly world, you more or less do it yourself. Heather has named her bedrooms (with power showers) after wild flowers, and gone in for bright colours, stained wood and stencilling. From her CRM office, she radiates a welcoming, warm efficiency, and produces delicious breakfasts from her kitchen.

~

NEARBY Tralee, 10 miles (16 km); Dingle, 20 miles (32 km); Killarney, 30 miles (48 km); Mount Brandon.
LOCATION within walking distance of the sea, 1 mile out of Camp village; parking available
MEALS breakfast
PRICES rooms I£18-I£25pp; standard double I£32-I£50; breakfast included
ROOMS 5; 2 double, 1 twin, 1 with three singles, 1 with double and single; all with shower; all with phone, tv, radio, hairdrier, safe, central heating
FACILITIES terrace, garden
CREDIT CARDS V **CHILDREN** by arrangement **DISABLED** not possible **PETS** may be kept in car **CLOSED** end Oct to mid-Mar **PROPRIETOR** Heather Williams

Co Kerry

CARAGH LAKE

ARD-NA-SIDHE
~ LAKESIDE HOTEL ~

Caragh Lake, Killorglin, Co Kerry
TEL 066 9769105 FAX 066 9769282
E-MAIL khl@iol.ie

WHEN WE VISITED ARD-NA-SIDHE (Gaelic for Hill of the Fairies) there appeared to be no-one about. The lovely wooded prize-winning gardens, with paths leading down to little grassy areas by the lake where there are benches to sit on and dream, were deserted. Most of the guests, we were told, were out playing golf. These golfing hotels are left like the *Marie Celeste* during the day, and lucky non-golfers may have the place to themselves. This handsome Victorian stone house, festooned with creeper, was built by a Lady Gordon and is so romantic that you can be as fanciful as you like. It certainly feels as if there are fairies about; indeed, behind the house is a fairy hill, with passages said to lead to a large cave. But these little creatures do not like to be seen. All credit must be given to Killarney Hotels for keeping the house quite uncommercialized and unspoiled, and bringing in Roy Lancaster to advise them on the gardens. There are no facilities here, except natural ones. But guests are given complimentary use of the 25-metre pool and sauna at the group's nearby sister hotels. Bedrooms (spacious) are in the main house or in the converted stables (very quiet and tranquil); all have impressive antiques and fabrics Lady Gordon might well have chosen herself; excellent bathrooms. Staff wear charming spotted frocks.

~

NEARBY Killorglin, 4$\frac{1}{2}$ miles (7 km); Killarney, 21 miles (34 km); Dingle peninsula; golf.
LOCATION in lakeside gardens, 4$\frac{1}{2}$ miles (7 km) from Killorglin; parking available
MEALS breakfast, dinner
PRICES rooms I£67.50-I£78pp; standard double I£135-I£158; breakfast included; dinner I£28 **ROOMS** 20; 18 double/twin, 2 single; 18 with bath, 2 with shower; all with phone, hairdrier; reception safe; kettle on request; ironing room
FACILITIES gardens, terraces; boating; swimming-pool nearby
CREDIT CARDS AE, DC, MC, V **CHILDREN** not suitable **DISABLED** downstairs room **PETS** not accepted **CLOSED** 1 Oct to 1 May
PROPRIETOR Killarney Hotels **MANAGER** Kathleen Dowling

CO KERRY

CARAGH LAKE

CARAGH LODGE
~ COUNTRY HOTEL ~

Caragh Lake, Co Kerry
TEL 066 9769115 **FAX** 066 9769316
E-MAIL caraghl@iol.ie

AN EXCELLENT RESPONSE to this comfortable house from a recent visitor: 'Full of warmth, and a marvellously peaceful setting' on the edge of Caragh Lake. The 100-year-old house is furnished with antiques and log fires, it has a 300-yard lake frontage, and there are nine acres of parkland with a fine planting of rare and sub-tropical shrubs. You get views of some of Ireland's highest mountains, abundant facilities for relaxation, quick access to the sea and glorious sandy beaches: a heady combination attractive to a great many holidaymakers (including golfers) – so much so that seven new rooms have been built to satisfy demand.

Mary Gaunt, described by our reporter as 'lively and fun', took over in 1989. She thoroughly redecorated the public rooms, bedrooms and the previously rather drab annexe rooms, and has achieved some impressive results. As a consequence the hotel is now a happy combination of elegance and informality. Mary's excellent cooking – featuring seafood, wild salmon and local lamb – has earned high praise from recent visitors.

~

NEARBY Killarney, 15 miles (24 km); Ring of Kerry.
LOCATION 22 miles (35 km) NW of Killarney, one mile (1.5 km) off Ring of Kerry road, W of Killorglin; in 9-acre gardens and parkland, with ample car parking
MEALS full breakfast, dinner; restaurant licence
PRICES B&B I£49.50–I£66; suite I£99; dinner I£29.70
ROOMS 15; 13 double, 1 single, 1 suite; all with bath; all rooms have central heating
FACILITIES 2 sitting-rooms, dining-room; tennis, swimming in lake, fishing, boating, sauna, bicycles
CREDIT CARDS AE, MC, V
CHILDREN welcome over 7
DISABLED access easy – some ground-floor bedrooms
PETS not accepted
CLOSED mid-Oct to Easter
PROPRIETOR Mary Gaunt

CO KERRY

CASTLEGREGORY

THE SHORES COUNTRY HOUSE

~ COUNTRY GUEST-HOUSE ~

Cappatigue, Castlegregory, Co Kerry
TEL/FAX 066 7139196
E-MAIL theshores@tinet.ie

W E HEARD GLOWING REPORTS of The Shores – on the north side of the
Dingle peninsula – on our travels, and of farmer's wife Annette
O'Mahony's passion for looking after guests. She has recently more or less
rebuilt her house to add on three extra rooms so that she can get her
hands on some more people to cosset. The setting for the house is
fabulous: just over the road in front is the 26-mile long sandy Brandon Bay
beach; in five minutes, you can be in the sea. Towering up behind is Mt
Brandon, the second highest mountain in Ireland. All rooms have sea
views. One has its own balcony; there's a long balcony, too, for general use.
And there's a library. Annette takes, as she says, "exceptional pride" in the
interior decorating of the house, and there are all kinds of charming
details in her rooms, such as writing desks, porcelain dolls, Laura Ashley
papers and fabrics, cream and white bedlinen. Her style could loosely be
described as Victorian. In her new cherry wood kitchen she makes porter
cake to accompany a welcome cup of tea on arrival, scrambles eggs and
pours maple syrup over waffles for breakfast. Milk is from the farm. For
dinner, there might well be beef raised on O'Mahony pastures, fresh
salmon, prawns in garlic butter. Flasks of coffee and packed lunches hold
you over through the day.

~

NEARBY Tralee; Dingle; Killarney; golf at Ballybunion.
LOCATION in gardens, 1 mile (1.6 km) W of Stradbally on Connor Pass; parking
available
MEALS breakfast, packed lunch, dinner
PRICES rooms I£22pp; standard double I£44: breakfast included; packed lunch
I£2.50; dinner I£15.50
ROOMS 6; 3 double, 2 twin,1 triple; 3 with bath; 3 with shower; all with phone, tv,
radio, hairdrier, tea/coffee making facilities
FACILITIES garden; sitting-room
CREDIT CARDS all major **CHILDREN** welcome **DISABLED** downstairs room **PETS** not
accepted **CLOSED** 30 Nov to 1 Feb **PROPRIETOR** Annette O'Mahony

CO CORK

BARNABROW HOUSE
~ COUNTRY HOUSE AND RESTAURANT ~

Cloyne, Midleton, Co Cork
TEL/FAX 021 652534
E-MAIL barnabrow@tinet.ie

OPENED TWO YEARS AGO at the back gate, as it were, of nearby Ballymaloe, this could be called a 'cutting edge' country house. No faded chintzes or family portraits here. Semi-minimalist interiors, with bold, bright colours, modern design and vast expanses of gleaming wood floors look as if they have come out of glossy magazines. So many guests ask how they can achieve the Barnabrow look that owner/chef Geraldine O'Brien has a list of suppliers ready. The flooring, one learns, is teak from environmentally managed forests in Zimbabwe and the pointed, cone-shaped lamps in the restaurant can be bought in Cork. Behind the rejuvenated 17thC main house is a coach house with floors painted white and elsewhere much orange, pink and yellow; a rustic stone cottage; and restaurant with an outdoor timber terrace. It all looks rather new and waiting to be weathered, but already, according to John O'Brien, who makes furniture, it has been voted one of the best B & Bs *in the world* by a TV holiday programme, and attracts an ever-growing band of discerning regulars, among them academics from Trinity College, Dublin. Hens that are very free-range provide fresh eggs; organic produce for the table comes from the kitchen garden; Barnabrow even has its own spring for lashings of crystal-clear water.

~

NEARBY Youghal; Cork.
LOCATION in 40 acres of gardens and woodland; parking available
MEALS breakfast, lunch, dinner
PRICES rooms I£30-I£45pp; standard double I£60; breakfast included; lunch I£5-I£12; dinner I£22
ROOMS 19; 11 double, 4 twin, 4 family rooms; 2 with bath, 17 with shower; all with phone, hairdrier
FACILITIES garden, terraces, children's playground
CREDIT CARDS MC, V
CHILDREN welcome **DISABLED** ground-floor rooms **PETS** accepted if well-behaved
CLOSED Christmas week **PROPRIETOR** Geraldine O'Brien

CO CORK

CORK

SEVEN NORTH MALL
~ TOWNHOUSE ~

7 North Mall, Cork, Co Cork
TEL 021 397191 **FAX** 021 300811
E-MAIL sevennorthmall@tinet.ie

ALTHOUGH THE LOCATION – in the centre of Cork – might seem hard to find, the one-way system through the city leads, magically, to North Mall, a row of elegant townhouses in a leafy terrace overlooking the River Lee. No. 7 – a tall, mid-18thC listed house – is charming, and perfectly placed for walking to restaurants, art galleries, theatres and the wealth of other attractions this lively city has to offer. (A useful map is provided.) Another major asset is secure parking in the private courtyard through the archway. There is no sign outside the house to spoil the gracious face it presents to the world. The Hegartys found it in a derelict state and have taken great care in the restoration: any original feature that could be kept has been. Angela Hegarty, whose hand is everywhere, likes proper bathrooms with deep baths, windows and fresh air, blankets on beds, wainscotting, stripped wood floors and attention to detail. She squeezes the oranges for fresh juice at breakfast, grinds the Java coffee beans, serves tea in teapots, and comes to the table herself to take orders. Scrambled eggs are cooked precisely as you would like them and are beautifully presented on plates from the East Cork pottery of Stephen Pearce. It is advisable to book ahead in order to avoid disappointment. Not surprisingly, this place has a cult following.

~

NEARBY city centre; university; Cork airport; Cork ferry terminal.
LOCATION riverside townhouse; parking available
MEALS breakfast
PRICES rooms I£35pp; standard double I£70; breakfast included
ROOMS 7; 5 double, 1 twin, 1 single; 6 with bath, 1 with shower; all with phone, tv, radio, hairdrier, trouser press
FACILITIES sitting-room; terrace
CREDIT CARDS MC, V
CHILDREN over-12s welcome
DISABLED 1 room possible **PETS** not in bedrooms; may be left in car
CLOSED 15 Dec to 6 Jan **PROPRIETORS** the Hegarty family

CO CORK

DINGLE

PAX HOUSE
~ GUEST-HOUSE ~

Upper John Street, Dingle, Co Kerry
TEL 066 9151518 **FAX** 066 9152461
E-MAIL paxhouse@iol.ie

THERE IS AN ABUNDANCE of wild fuchsia in the hedgerows of the little lanes around Pax House, high on a green hill looking down over Dingle Bay. Before breakfast, you can take an early walk down to the shore, or, from the terrace, count the cows coming out of the milking parlour of the farm below this rather odd building that was once a retirement home. Joan Brosnan-Wright, a former Stoke Mandeville nurse, and her husband, Ron, who was a BBC engineer, have transformed the place to provide a series of comfortable bedrooms decorated with an early Celtic theme. Joan has used letters from the Ogham alphabet – the earliest form of written Irish used around the 4thC AD and found on standing stones – to decorate curtains, monastic parchment shades on bedside lamps and Donegal woollen blankets on beds. Most rooms have showers; cold taps produce water from the Wrights' own spring well. From the dining-room, where Joan serves her delicious home-made breads (try the white almond or the brown fruit for breakfast) you can see the field on SleaHead that starred in a film with Tom Cruise, and over to the Ring of Kerry. The silence on the green hill is blissful, but Dingle, a swinging little town, with its full share of traditional music, pubs and restaurants, much frequented by celebs, is only a short walk away.

~

NEARBY Killarney, 42 miles (68 km); Mount Brandon; Tralee, 30 miles (48 km).
LOCATION in countryside, half a mile (0.8 km) out of Dingle town; signposted on N86; parking available
MEALS breakfast
PRICES rooms I£25pp; standard double I£50; breakfast included
ROOMS 13; 8 double, 4 double and single, 1 single; 5 with bath, 8 with shower; all with phone, tv, radio, hairdrier, trouser press, tea/coffee making facilities
FACILITIES terraces
CREDIT CARDS AE, MC, V
CHILDREN 1 family at a time **DISABLED** not possible **PETS** if well-behaved
CLOSED never **PROPRIETORS** Joan and Ron Brosnan-Wright

CO KERRY

DINGLE

DOYLE'S SEAFOOD RESTAURANT

~ RESTAURANT WITH ROOMS ~

John Street, Dingle, Co Kerry
TEL 066 51174 **FAX** 066 51816

'MOST ATTRACTIVE AND UNEXPECTED,' says one of our most experienced inspectors. 'A charming homey feeling – they give you your own door key.' It is in fact a delightful, small hotel in the middle of a quaint fishing village on the Dingle Peninsula. The visitors' book perches on an antique writing-desk in the elegant sitting-room; it drips with superlatives, and rightly so.

Sean and Charlotte Cluskey have recently taken over from the Doyles, who originally gave their name to the place over two decades ago when they moved to this wild and lovely corner of Kerry. Eight spacious bedrooms and a sitting-room were added next door to the restaurant when the neighbouring house came on the market. The bedrooms are all beautifully decorated: the four back rooms have balconies looking over the tiny garden, and the two downstairs rooms (suitable for disabled guests) open on to it. Fresh flowers and potted plants abound throughout.

The restaurant is as popular and cosmopolitan as ever, and it is easy to see why. The menu is mainly, but not exclusively, fishy, and changes with the seasons. By all accounts the food really is superb, and pretty good value, too. We welcome more reports.

~

NEARBY Dingle Peninsula; Ring of Kerry; (beaches, historical sites.
LOCATION just off main street of town; with small garden and on-street parking
MEALS breakfast, lunch, dinner; full licence
PRICES B&B I£38-I£40; dinner I£21
ROOMS 8; 8 double, all with bath; all rooms have central heating, phone, tv, hairdrier, radio
FACILITIES dining-room, sitting-room
CREDIT CARDS DC, MC, V
CHILDREN welcome; baby-sitting by arrangement
DISABLED 2 ground-floor bedrooms
PETS not accepted
CLOSED mid-Nov to mid-Mar **PROPRIETORS** Sean and Charlotte Cluskey

Co Cork

LEIGHMONEYMORE
~ FARMHOUSE BED-AND-BREAKFAST ~

Dunderrow, Kinsale, Co Cork
TEL 021 775312 **FAX** 021 775692

BELGIAN-BORN DOMINIQUE O'SULLIVAN-VERVAET is one of a dynamic breed of young women who manage effortlessly to juggle their various roles: she is farmer's wife, mother, and all-round provider to travellers. In her neat navy-blue skirt she bustles about dispensing delicious breakfasts from her Aga and looking after guests, conversing all the while. Her blonde-haired children play at her feet and she has a natural gift for making everyone feel cherished. The bright, tiled conservatory attached to the house acts as a kind of communal sitting area. As there is always something going on in her presence, her husband, Michael, has difficulty staying outside getting on with his farming tasks. Cups of tea and coffee are constantly being served by Dominique, and guests have as much difficulty as Michael in setting off on their outing of the day because they are enjoying themselves so much and are minded to stay put. There are dogs and cats and peacocks, chickens and geese and beef cattle. The pretty bedrooms have floral themes: curtains and wallpapers are sprigged and there are fresh flowers from the garden. She hides away the TV sets because she doesn't like the look of them, and certainly, the place is so congenial that one wonders if guests ever give TV a second's thought.

~

NEARBY Kinsale, 3$\frac{1}{2}$ miles (6 km); Cork , 18 miles (29 km).
LOCATION on 50-acre farm on banks of River Bandon; parking available
MEALS breakfast
PRICES rooms I£25pp; standard double I£50; breakfast included
ROOMS 5; 3 double, 2 family; all with bath; all rooms have phone, tv, hairdrier
FACILITIES garden, terrace; riverside walks
CREDIT CARDS MC, V
CHILDREN welcome
DISABLED not possible
PETS by arrangement
CLOSED 1 Nov to mid-Mar
PROPRIETOR Dominique O'Sullivan-Vervaet

Co Limerick

Glin

Glin Castle
~ Heritage house ~

Glin, Co Limerick
Tel 068 34173/34112 **Fax** 068 34364
e-mail knight@iol.ie

ONE OF THE OUTSTANDING private houses of the world, this is the home of the 29th Knight of Glin, who represents Christie's in Ireland, and his wife who bears the charming title of Madam FitzGerald. On the banks of the Shannon, it is dreamy and beautiful, in pale stone and with castellations. As might be imagined with a title that goes back to the 14thC, it is filled with family history and lovely family things. Even when the Knight is at the castle, guests have the run of the house and garden. Friendly young staff are endlessly attentive. Glin exudes grace, and manages to be both grand and intimate at the same time. The entrance hall, which may have been used as a ballroom in the past, has Corinthian pillars and a plaster ceiling apparently untouched since the1780s. In the reception rooms is a unique collection of Irish 18thC mahogany furniture. To go to bed, you take the flying staircase – the only one of its kind in Ireland – to the first floor. Some rooms here have four-poster beds, and all have fabulous bathrooms.

You may tag along behind one of the guided parties to learn all about the place. A cosy little private sitting-room for guests has deep pink sofas round the fire, family photographs and after-dinner coffee. Be sure to make time for a walk to the walled garden.

~

Nearby Limerick, 32 miles (51 km); golf at Ballybunion; Ring of Kerry.
Location on 400-acre estate, with gardens and farm, on river's edge; parking available
Meals breakfast, dinner
Prices rooms I£85-I£135pp; standard double I£170; dinner I£27.50
Rooms 15; 14 double; 1 twin; 2 with dressing-rooms; all with bath and shower; all rooms with phone, tv, hairdrier; safe at reception; all with room service
Facilities formal gardens; woodland; tennis court **Credit cards** AE, DC, MC, V
Children accepted; baby-sitting arranged; cots provided **Disabled** not possible
Pets kennels provided **Closed** end of Nov to Feb
Proprietors Desmond and Olda FitzGerald **Manager** Bob Duff

Co Cork

GOLEEN

FORTVIEW HOUSE

~ FARMHOUSE BED-AND-BREAKFAST ~

Gurtyowen, Toormore, Goleen, Co Cork
TEL/FAX 028 35324

THIS PLACE IS A LABOUR OF LOVE, and it radiates an appropriately warm glow. Richard Connell built the newer part of this house on the West Cork family dairy farm himself, out of stone, and roofed it in slate. The interior is the inspired work of his delightful wife, Violet. With her own ideas, and pictures from magazines, she has created something so fresh, welcoming and comfortable that it is hard to tear oneself away. You can tell what's in store by the two small bears in the retro pram in the hall and the boxy blue-and-red chairs in the sitting room. Violet's bedrooms are named after wild flowers: periwinkle; lavender; daffodil; fuchsia. In one, she has hung straw hats on the wall. She has made curtains out of striped mattress ticking and stencilled a bathroom with sea shells. In a family room with two single beds and pretty patchwork quilts, she props teddy bears up on the pillows as if they are waiting for new, young friends to come. The beamed dining-room has a long table, terracotta tiles, wood-burning stove, and old pine furniture. Violet's breakfasts reflect the same attention and care: eggs from the Connell's own hens; freshly squeezed juices; hot potato cakes, salmon and crème fraîche. She already has many admirers. Be sure to book early.

~

NEARBY Goleen; Mizen Head; Schull peninsula; Skibbereen; Bantry.
LOCATION in countryside, 6 miles (10 km) from Goleen; parking available
MEALS breakfast
PRICES rooms I£25pp; standard double I£50; breakfast included
ROOMS 5; 2 with 2 double, 2 with double and single, 1 with double and 2 single; 1 with bath, 4 with shower; all rooms with hairdrier
FACILITIES garden, terrace; tea and coffee served in sitting-room
CREDIT CARDS not accepted
CHILDREN over 6 welcome
DISABLED not possible
PETS not accepted
CLOSED 1 Nov to 1 Mar **PROPRIETOR** Violet Connell

Co Cork

GOLEEN

THE HERON'S COVE

~ RESTAURANT WITH ROOMS ~

Goleen, Co Cork
TEL 028 35225 **FAX** 028 35422
E-MAIL suehill@tinet.ie

A FISHERMAN IN A TRAWLER brings Sue Hill's order to the door of her white-painted, waterside restaurant, which offers 'fresh fish and wine on the harbour' and, most likely, a view of a heron. It is an idyllic spot, on this rugged stretch of the West Cork coastline. It is not surprising to hear from Sue that some of her guests do not want to do anything but simply sit and watch the tide come in and go out again. Three of the bedrooms in this modern house open on to balconies overlooking the little sheltered cove, and from the terrace of the restaurant on the ground floor – which is open from May to October – there are steps down to the beach. Guests are clearly those who relish the peace and quiet. Along the upstairs landing runs a long shelf with a row of books. Bedrooms are well-equipped – some of the pillowcases may not match, but this might not be too important. There are posters of Aix-en-Provence on the walls and Sue has turned the staircase into a gallery for local artists. She is also very switched on to IT and offers guests e-mail and fax facilities. It's only a short walk to the village of Goleen and Sue sends all visitors off on the spectacular drive to Mizen Head, which is Ireland's most southwesterly point.

~

NEARBY Mizen Head; Cork, 75 miles (120 km); Bantry, 25 miles (40 km); Skibbereen, 24 miles (39 km).
LOCATION on Goleen Harbour; parking available
MEALS breakfast, lunch, dinner
PRICES rooms I£25pp sea view; I£18pp side view; standard double I£50; breakfast included; lunch from I£5; dinner I£19.50
ROOMS 5; 1 double, 2 twin, 2 double with a single bed; 1 with bath, 4 with shower; all with phone, tv, hairdrier, electric blanket, tea/coffee making facilities
FACILITIES terraces, garden
CREDIT CARDS AE, MC, V **CHILDREN** by arrangement
DISABLED not possible
PETS not accepted
CLOSED Christmas week **PROPRIETOR** Sue Hill

CO CORK

INNISHANNON

INNISHANNON HOUSE
~ COUNTRY HOTEL ~

Innishannon, Co Cork
TEL 021 775121 **FAX** 021 775609

CONAL O'SULLIVAN RETURNED to his Irish roots in 1989 when he and his wife Vera moved to this attractive, imposing 18thC house on the banks of the Bandon river. The couple are seasoned hoteliers and travellers, having run hotels all over the world (their last stop the Caribbean) but they are particularly excited at this latest challenge.

The hotel has already become a welcoming haven for visitors, its comfortable, attractive rooms hung with the O'Sullivans' extensive collection of modern art (including two possible Gauguins in the dining-room). Vera has a great eye for interior design, and has decorated all the bedrooms with infinite care and flair – number 16 is a cosy attic room with an antique bedspread, number 14 a fascinating circular room with small round windows and a huge curtained bed. Irish hero, Michael Collins' bath is the latest addition to the antiques around the hotel – to join that of Winston Churchill. The enormous suite has a Victorian bathroom.

The O'Sullivan's son, Pearse, does the cooking, with emphasis on seafood, lobster and seasonal produce. Dinner in the lovely pink dining-room is a gastronomic delight. Pre-dinner drinks are served outside in summer, or in the airy lounge, or cosy bar – full of photos of Conal's car rallying days. Innishannon is not the last word in seclusion or intimacy; there are facilities for conferences and wedding receptions.

~

NEARBY Kinsale, 7 miles (11 km); Cork, 15 miles (24 km)
LOCATION on banks of river, near village; with gardens and car parking
MEALS breakfast, lunch, dinner, snacks
PRICES B&B I£50-I£95; dinner from I£25; weekly and off-season reductions
ROOMS 13; 7double, 6 twin; all with bath and shower; all rooms have central heating, phone, tv, hairdrier
FACILITIES dining-room, sitting-room, bar, terrace; fishing, boating
CREDIT CARDS AE, DC, MC, V **CHILDREN** welcome **DISABLED** ground-floor suite
PETS accepted in bedrooms only **CLOSED** mid-Jan to mid-Mar
PROPRIETORS Conal and Vera O'Sullivan

Co Cork

ASSOLAS COUNTRY HOUSE

~ COUNTRY HOUSE HOTEL ~

Kanturk, Co Cork
TEL 029 50015 **FAX** 029 50795
E-MAIL assolas@tinet.ie

THIS HISTORIC, mellow country house, in a fairy-tale setting of award-winning gardens beside a slow-flowing river, has been in the Bourke family since the early years of this century. The familiar story of escalating maintenance costs and dwindling bank balances led to their taking in guests in 1966, and since then they have never looked back. Assolas is still their family home, and the business of sharing it has obviously turned out to be a pleasure. One recent visitor described her stay there as 'stunning, with wonderful, beautifully served food'.

The house was built around 1590, and had unusual circular extensions added at two corners in Queen Anne's time; beyond the expanses of lawn are mature woods, and then hills and farmland. Inside, the public rooms are richly decorated and elegantly furnished, almost entirely with antiques, and immaculately kept. The bedrooms are notably spacious and many have large luxury bathrooms – the 'circular' rooms at the corners of the house are particularly impressive. Three of the rooms are in a renovated stone building in the courtyard. The food, prepared by Hazel Bourke, is in what might be called modern Irish style – country cooking of fresh ingredients (many home-grown).

~

NEARBY Killarney (Ring of Kerry); Limerick; Blarney.
LOCATION 12 miles (19 km) W of Mallow, NE of Kanturk, signposted from N72; in extensive gardens with ample car parking
MEALS full breakfast, light or packed lunch, dinner; full licence
PRICES B&B I£55-I£84; dinner I£32; reductions for children under 12 sharing
ROOMS 9 double/family rooms; all with bath and shower; all rooms have central heating, phone
FACILITIES sitting-room, dining-room; fishing, tennis, boating, croquet
CREDIT CARDS AE, DC, MC, V **Children** welcome
DISABLED access fair **PETS** welcome, but must stay in stables
CLOSED Nov to Apr (except by prior arrangement)
PROPRIETORS the Bourke family

Co Kerry

MUXNAW LODGE
~ BED-AND-BREAKFAST ~

Castletownbere Road, Kenmare, Co Kerry
TEL 064 41252

KENMARE IS A MARKET TOWN at the head of the sheltered Kenmare River estuary, with some handsome 19thC buildings. A popular tourist centre, it has two busy main streets with plenty of shops with painted fronts selling woollen goods, and two of the best hotels in Ireland. It is a perfect kicking-off point for the road around the gorgeous Ring of Kerry, which, in the summer, can become a long traffic jam, with nose-to-tail coaches. Allow a day for it, and set up base camp at charming, gabled Muxnaw Lodge, built in 1801, one of the oldest houses in the town, set on a hillside overlooking the suspension bridge. Hannah Boland has created an attractive period style for her lovely old house, with dark Laura Ashley wallpapers with little prints, brass beds and lovingly-polished antique furniture. In the bedrooms, she hides the modern electric kettles away in wooden boxes so they don't spoil the general look. In a bathroom at the back of the house, you may sit in the corner bath and look at the sea. Breakfasts include yoghurt with honey; fresh eggs from the butcher are cooked on Mrs Boland's big red Aga in the kitchen. Her apple tart is a resounding success at dinner. She is such a delightful hostess that guests may find themselves getting away rather later than planned on that trip around the Ring of Kerry.

~

NEARBY Ring of Kerry; Beara peninsula; Killarney; Bantry Bay.
LOCATION overlooking bay and suspension bridge; 10 minutes walk to town centre; parking available
MEALS breakfast, dinner on request
PRICES rooms I£22pp; standard double I£44; breakfast included; dinner I£15
ROOMS 5; 3 double, 2 twin; 2 with bath, 3 with shower; all rooms with tv, radio, hairdrier, tea/coffee making facilities; trouser press available
FACILITIES garden, terrace; all-weather tennis court
CREDIT CARDS not accepted
CHILDREN welcome **DISABLED** not possible **PETS** welcome outside **CLOSED** Christmas
PROPRIETOR Hannah Boland

CO CORK

KINSALE

THE OLD BANK HOUSE
~ TOWN GUEST-HOUSE ~

11 Pearse Street, Kinsale, Co Cork
TEL 021 774075 **FAX** 021 774296

KINSALE, ONCE AN UNSPOILED seaside village, is now a major resort often called the 'gourmet capital' of Ireland. To escape from the noise and the crowds, what a relief it is to step into the serenity of this tall Georgian townhouse, right in the centre, that used to belong to a bank. Looking after You is the priority here. Assistant manager Noel Fletcher sleeps on the premises and there is that rarity, night service. The place is owned by well-known Kinsale chef Michael Riese and his wife, Marie. One of the first things they did on acquiring the house was to put in a lift so that guests do not have to struggle with luggage up and down the stairs – there are seven flights of them. Michael cooks breakfast in his professional chef's kitchen. A curious small dining-room has exposed stone walls and raftered ceiling. The charmingly cluttered sitting-room has well-thumbed restaurant guides and a hospitality tray. Upstairs, there are orthopaedic beds, Noel's little bunker of an office, and an air of plush comfort. Each room has a superb bathroom. Everything that's done is done well. Bed linen is crisp and white; there are brass light switches. Double glazing gives an undisturbed night; a single key opens all doors if you stay out late. Parking can be a bit of a problem, but Noel obligingly goes and reserves spaces for cars right outside the front of the house.

~

NEARBY Cork, 15 miles (24 km); Blarney Stone, 20 miles (32 km); Bantry Bay, 45 miles (72 km); golf.
LOCATION in town centre; parking available by arrangement
MEALS breakfast
PRICES rooms I£55-I£85pp; standard double I£110; breakfast included
ROOMS 17; 14 double/twin, 3 family; all with bath and power shower; all rooms with phone, tv, radio, hairdrier; some with trouser press; kettles, ironing boards on request
FACILITIES lift **CREDIT CARDS** all major
CHILDREN by arrangement **DISABLED** not possible **PETS** not accepted
CLOSED 3 days at Christmas **PROPRIETORS** Marie and Michael Riese

Co Cork

PERRYVILLE HOUSE
~ GUEST-HOUSE ~

Kinsale, Co Cork
TEL 021 772731 **FAX** 021 772298

MAYBE, BY NOW, owner Laura Corcoran will have managed to have this handsome 19thC house on the water's edge painted the pink of her desires – a little paler and not so bright. But whatever the exterior colour, what Perryville House has in spades is acres of space. The light, airy rooms go on forever and there seem to be miles of lovely pale natural seagrass matting on the wide staircase and landings that lead to deep windows with views of harbour, sky and seagulls. It rather goes to one's head, like champagne, in the most pleasurable of ways. This is a most civilized haven of peace and luxurious comfort for those in need of a retreat. Sinatra sets the mood as you come in from the street to see welcoming sofas and blazing fires. Enormous bathrooms immediately tempt you to indulge yourself, with piles of fluffy white towels (fluffy white towelling dressing-gowns, too, in superior rooms), water gushing out of the taps, and heated towel rails, even a second telephone. Beds are high and wide, with crisp white sheets, satin-bound blankets and somewhere, miles away across the wide open spaces of the room, a huge cupboard or an antique chair. Eight more of these pleasing rooms are to come soon in the building next door. Generous breakfast; morning coffee; afternoon tea. Parking is opposite the front door.

~

NEARBY Cork; Cork airport; golf at Kinsale Old Head.
LOCATION on waterside, in centre of Kinsale, on Cork road; parking available
MEALS breakfast
PRICES per room; standard room I£120; superior room I£160; breakfast included
ROOMS 22; 19 double, 3 twin; all with bath and shower; all with phone, tv, hairdrier
FACILITIES terrace, small courtyard; sitting-rooms
CREDIT CARDS AE, DC, MC, V
CHILDREN not under 12
DISABLED 3 downstairs rooms
PETS not accepted
CLOSED end Oct to 10 Mar **PROPRIETORS** Laura Corcoran and Barry McDermott

Co Cork

LONGUEVILLE HOUSE
~ COUNTRY HOUSE HOTEL ~

Mallow, Co Cork
TEL 022 47156/47306 FAX 022 47459
E-MAIL longuevillehouse.ie

ONE OF THE FINEST country house hotels in Ireland: this elegant and imposing pink listed Georgian house on a 500-acre wooded estate on the Blackwater River has a three-storey block in the centre built in the 1720s, later wings, and a pretty Victorian conservatory. Inside, it is full of ornate Italian plasterwork, elaborately framed ancestral oils and graceful period furniture. The drawing-room overlooks lawns and rows of oaks in the parkland; in the distance are the ruins of the O'Callaghans' Dromineen Castle, demolished under Cromwell, who dispossessed the family. But, after 300 years, they are back. Longueville House has everything, including internationally-recognized chef William O'Callaghan, who, according to one leading food critic, cooks 'some of the finest food in Europe'. Many of his ingredients come from the estate farm, and he also produces a white wine from his own vineyard. Bedrooms are comfortable and filled with antiques. The ones at the front of the house have the best views. A recent visitor says the O'Callaghans are 'charming and informal', and it is very easy to feel relaxed in their beautiful house. The Presidents' Restaurant is named after the portraits of Irish presidents that hang on the walls. The wine list is superb, as is William's seven-course Surprise Tasting Menu.

~

NEARBY Mallow Castle; Anne's Grove Gardens at Castletownroche.
LOCATION on wooded estate, 3 miles (5 km) W of Mallow on Killarney road; ample parking
MEALS breakfast, dinner
PRICES rooms I£136-I£166; standard double I£156; breakfast included; dinner I£31
ROOMS 20; 13 double/twin with bath; 7 suites; all with central heating, tv, radio, phone, hairdrier **FACILITIES** sitting-room, drawing-room, bar, 2 dining-rooms; billiards, table-tennis; fishing **CREDIT CARDS** all major **CHILDREN** welcome
DISABLED easy access to public rooms only **PETS** not accepted
CLOSED Christmas to mid-Feb **PROPRIETORS** the O'Callaghan family

Co Cork

BALLYMALOE HOUSE
∼ COUNTRY HOUSE HOTEL ∼

Shanagarry, Midleton, Co Cork
TEL 021 652531 **FAX** 021 652021

THIRTY BEDROOMS NORMALLY rules out a hotel for this guide, but we cannot resist this amiable, rambling, creeper-clad house – largely Georgian in appearance but incorporating the remains of a 14thC castle keep – set in rolling green countryside. Visitors in 1998 were 'immensely impressed' and found the staff 'as well-drilled as an army, but jolly, with abundant charm'.

The Allens, who have been farming here for over 40 years, opened as a restaurant in 1964 and started offering rooms three years later. Since then they have added more facilities and more rooms – those in the main house now outnumbered by those in extensions and converted out-buildings.

Despite quite elegant and sophisticated furnishings, the Allens have always managed to preserve intact the warmth and naturalness of a much-loved family home. But not all visitors agree: one reporter judged that Ballymaloe was becoming rather commercialized. Even that reporter, however, was impressed by the standard of food. Mrs Allen no longer takes an active role in the cooking. It is now Rory O'Connell who prepares the Classic French and Irish dishes alongside original dishes, all based on home produce and fish fresh from the local quays. (Sunday dinner is always a buffet.) Just as much care is lavished on breakfast, and the famous children's high tea.

∼

NEARBY beaches, cliff walks, fishing, golf.
LOCATION 20 miles (32 km) E of Cork, 2 miles (3 km) E of Cloyne on the Ballycotton road, L35 **MEALS** breakfast, lunch, dinner; full licence
PRICES B&B I£60-I£100; dinner I£34.50; bargain breaks Nov to mid-Mar
ROOMS 33; 33 double/twin; 31 with bath, 2 with shower; all have central heating, phone **FACILITIES** 3 sitting-rooms, conference/TV room, conservatory, library; tennis, golf, heated outdoor swimming-pool (summer) **CREDIT CARDS** AE, DC, MC, V **CHILDREN** welcome; high tea provided **DISABLED** access easy; some rooms built for wheelchairs **PETS** tolerated – not in bedrooms/public rooms **CLOSED** over Christmas **PROPRIETORS** I and M Allen

Co Cork

LETTERCOLLUM HOUSE

~ COUNTRY GUEST-HOUSE AND RESTAURANT ~

Timoleague, Co Cork
TEL 023 46251 **FAX** 023 46270
E-MAIL conmc@iol.ie

THE PERIODICALS IN THE SITTING-ROOM say much about this quirky yellow brick Victorian house with blue windows: *Cycling; The Telegraph Magazine; Amnesty*. It used to be a convent; what was the chapel, with stained glass windows and confessional box, is now the restaurant. The hall is painted green and yellow with a enormous plant sitting on a chunky hand-made oak table in primitive style. A splendid staircase, with stone steps and wrought-iron banister, leads to the upper floors. Everything is a little bit eccentric – and all the more enjoyable for it. Lettercollum was going to be an alternative artistic community until, as is often the way, the friends split up. Some still live in the stable block; their work, such as pictures, lamp fittings and special decorative paint effects, makes up the colourful, off-beat character of the house. Chefs/proprietors Karen Austin and Con McLoughlin have gone it alone: a talented couple, their cooking is sophisticated and their hospitality relaxed and easy-going. There's a lovingly-tended organic kitchen garden, home-grown pigs, local free-range eggs, and plenty of vegetarian specials on the menu. The large, airy bedrooms have paintwork in bold colours; most have showers. Children are made especially welcome. Parents can relax while eating a meal in the restaurant, watching their offspring play outside.

NEARBY Courtmacsherry Bay; Kinsale; Clonakilty, 6 miles (10 km); Cork, 32 miles (51 km).
LOCATION in 12 acres of woodland and pasture, 1 mile (1.6 km) from Timoleague; parking available
MEALS breakfast, lunch on Sunday only, dinner
PRICES rooms I£20-I£30pp; standard double I£52; breakfast included; dinner I£21
ROOMS 9 (2 in annexe); 4 double, 2 with a double and single, 3 with double and 2 single; 1 with bath, 8 with shower; all with phone, tea/coffee making facilities; hairdrier on request **FACILITIES** gardens; restaurant **CREDIT CARDS** AE, DC, MC, V
CHILDREN welcome **DISABLED** not possible **PETS** not accepted
CLOSED Nov-Mar **PROPRIETORS** Karen Austin and Con McLoughlin

Co Cork

AHERNE'S SEAFOOD RESTAURANT

~ RESTAURANT WITH ROOMS ~

163 North Main Street, Youghal, Co Cork
TEL 024 92424 **FAX** 024 93633
E-MAIL ahernes@tinet.ie

THIS BUSY, PICTURESQUE, walled port at the mouth of the Blackwater River in East Cork makes one want to adapt Dr Johnson's comment about London: if a man is tired of Youghal, he is tired of life. In the heart of it all is Aherne's, a family-run, renowned 'gourmet landmark' specializing in the freshest of seafood caught in the bountiful fishing grounds off the coast. You may well see dinner arriving off the trawlers down on the quay. If you book in here, you can stay up as late you like with the locals in the bars, or the restaurant, and simply go up to bed to what have been described as rooms with a 'seafood view'. You will be surprised at what you find: luxurious, generous-sized bedrooms with massive beds and good antique furniture; a cosy little library with chairs and sofas gathered round an inviting turf fire, with bookshelves on each side. Prints of ornamental chickens hang in the corridor; with thick carpets it's all very quiet and relaxing after the hustle and bustle of the streets. Bonus points must be given to the FitzGibbon family (now on the third generation) for thinking of everything, even balconies to some of the rooms, giving guests a chance to sit out when weather permits, and, in a town that has much traffic in high season, for the secure, private parking in the courtyard.

NEARBY Blackwater Estuary; Cork, 30 miles (48 km); Waterford, 45 miles (72 km).
LOCATION in town centre; parking available
MEALS breakfast, lunch, dinner
PRICES rooms I£60-I£80pp; standard double I£120; breakfast included; lunch from I£16; dinner I£28.50
ROOMS 12; all double; all rooms with bath, phone, tv, radio, hairdrier, trouser press
FACILITIES drawing-room; library
CREDIT CARDS all major
CHILDREN welcome
DISABLED possible **PETS** not accepted
CLOSED 5 days at Christmas **PROPRIETOR** David FitzGibbon

CO WATERFORD

ARDMORE

BYRON LODGE
~ VILLAGE GUEST-HOUSE ~

Ardmore, Co Waterford
TEL 024 94157

A RDMORE IS A DELIGHTFUL VILLAGE on its own peninsula with a long sandy beach, narrow streets with painted houses and numerous restaurants. It has a famous round tower built by early Christian monks where they stored their valuables during Viking raids. Ardmore was also the home of novelist Molly Keane (died 1996), who, writing of her Irish Ascendancy background, said there was always 'an absolute duty to be amusing'. She was a friend of Mary Byron Casey, who has such a wealth of stories to tell about Ardmore and her life and travels that staying with her in what used to be her family's holiday house is highly entertaining. She loves her guests and says she is miserable without them. Her house is rarely empty, though, because she has a faithful band of followers who make a point of returning again and again to Byron Lodge, with its red front door, pretty garden, Mary's warm welcome (a special one for small dogs), cups of tea and bargain prices. Everything here is simple and unpretentious. Rooms are spacious and comfortable, with a variety of bath/shower arrangements. Attic rooms on the top floor have marvellous sea views through dormer windows. The smell of home-baked bread comes from the kitchen; breakfast on 'house' mushroom or cheese omelettes made with free-range eggs.

~

NEARBY Waterford; Youghal; Powerscourt; Lismore; beaches.
LOCATION in Ardmore village, with gardens, overlooking beach and Ardmore Bay; parking available
MEALS breakfast, dinner by request
PRICES rooms I£15-I£18pp; standard double I£36; breakfast included; dinner I£12
ROOMS 6; 3 double, 1 twin, 2 with double and single; 4 with shower, 2 with bath; 2 share bathroom; hairdrier on request
FACILITIES garden, terrace; guided tours of area on request
CREDIT CARDS not accepted
CHILDREN welcome **DISABLED** no facilities **PETS** accepted **CLOSED** end Oct to 1 Apr
PROPRIETOR Mary Byron Casey

CO WATERFORD

BALLYMACARBRY, NIRE VALLEY

HANORA'S COTTAGE

~ RIVERSIDE GUEST-HOUSE ~

Glenanore, Ballymacarbry, Co Waterford
TEL 052 36134 **FAX** 052 36540

CHANGES HAVE TAKEN PLACE at award-winning Hanora's Cottage, built by a little bridge over the river in the beautiful Nire Valley for owner Seamus Wall's great-grandmother. With the village school and church next door, the picturesque group of buildings and their setting made our inspector think of somewhere in the Pyrenees. The guest-house is a favourite with walkers, who come for the Comeragh Mountains and nearby forests and lakes. Mary Wall puts comfort high on her list and pampers her guests. She has added five new rooms and a spa tub in a conservatory-with-views, where guests may rest aching limbs and emerge refreshed for a candlelit dinner in the new dining-room. Food is prepared by the Walls' talented Ballymaloe-trained son, Eoin. In the new extension, brilliantly designed to fit with the rest of the building, Mary has put in a drying and boot room. Bedrooms are large, calm and peaceful, with thick carpets, and most have spa baths (superiors have double Jacuzzis). There are books by the beds, some Tiffany lamps, and quality bedlinen. The breakfast-room looks out on to the little stone bridge and Seamus's home-baked gluten-free brown bread has an international reputation. Plenty of fruit and freshly-squeezed juices, too. Ask for a front room if you want to fall asleep to the sound of the river.

~

NEARBY Dungarvan, 18 miles (29 km); Clonmel, 15 miles (24 km); Blackwater Valley.
LOCATION in Nire Valley, 4 miles (6 km) out of Ballymacarbry; parking available
MEALS breakfast, packed lunch, dinner
PRICES rooms I£35-I£45pp; standard double I£70; breakfast included; dinner I£23
ROOMS 11; all double/twin; all with bath; all rooms with phone, tv, hairdrier; tea/coffee making facilities
FACILITIES garden, terrace; spa tub
CREDIT CARDS MC, V
CHILDREN not accepted **DISABLED** not possible **PETS** not accepted
CLOSED Christmas week **PROPRIETORS** Seamus and Mary Wall

Co Wexford

CAMPILE

KILMOKEA

~ COUNTRY MANOR AND GARDENS ~

Great Island, Campile, Co Wexford
TEL 051 388109 **FAX** 051 388776
E-MAIL kilmokea@indigo.ie

THIS IS A TRUE PARADISE for anyone who loves gardens. Emma Hewlett and her husband, Mark (an ex-policeman), are an enterprising young couple who came from London looking for a different kind of life, with horses. (At the time of writing, Mark was still commuting.) They found Kilmokea, a Georgian rectory in a spectacular and beautiful seven acres of gardens created over some 50 years by a Colonel and Mrs Price, which they lovingly maintain and open to the public. To be able to stay right in the middle of these exceptional gardens and have the run of them before breakfast, or last thing at night, is a rare treat and makes one feel quite privileged. The house had to be completely revamped to fit in the guest rooms, which if not large are pretty and comfortable, with super showers, generous supplies of towels, and views of lush greenery. One room has a four-poster; another a *bateau lit*. The Hewletts were getting into the swing of their new life when we visited: Tim had been on a Prue Leith cookery course; Emma, who works with a large staff, had really got to know her plants and Latin names tripped off her tongue. They were growing herbs for the kitchen and waiting for some hens to join the peacocks. You can eat lunch and cream tea in the large, airy conservatory. Ask about the giant borage.

~

NEARBY Waterford; Dunbrody Abbey; JFK Arboretum.
LOCATION in gardens, 9 miles (14 km) S of New Ross; parking available
MEALS breakfast, lunch, dinner
PRICES rooms I£45, I£55, I£65pp; standard double I£110; lunch from I£5; dinner I£25
ROOMS 4; 3 double, 1 twin; 2 with bath, 2 with shower; all with phone, hairdrier
FACILITIES garden, terrace, Italian loggia; tea-room; aromatherapy treatment
CREDIT CARDS AE, MC, V
CHILDREN welcome; cot
DISABLED not possible **PETS** not in house; kennels in yard **CLOSED** never
PROPRIETORS Mark and Emma Hewlett

CO TIPPERARY

CASHEL (CO TIPPERARY)

CASHEL PALACE HOTEL

~ CONVERTED BISHOP'S PALACE ~

Main Street, Cashel, Co Tipperary
TEL 062 62707 **FAX** 062 61521
E-MAIL reception@cashel-palace.ie

CHARM AND GRACE OOZES out of every pore of this exquisite 18thC former archbishop's palace in the historic market town of Cashel, with its famous and dramatic Rock, one of Ireland's most visited sites. The story is that the Devil, in a hurry to fly on his way, bit a chunk out of the Slieve Bloom Mountains and dropped it here. From right outside the hotel drawing-room you may follow the Bishop's Walk, which leads you through the delightful garden and a grassy meadow to the Rock and its cluster of grey ruins. In the garden are two mulberry trees planted in 1702 for the coronation of Queen Anne, and the descendents of the original hops planted by one of the Guinness family in the mid-18thC (there's plenty of the 'black', velvety stuff in the Guinness Bar, with flagged cellar floor and terracotta walls). We don't have enough room to sing all the praises of this jewel in the heart of racing country that used to be owned by trainer Vincent O'Brien; breakfast is served in the pine-panelled room named after him. There are four-poster beds, fine antiques and pictures, and spacious bathrooms – with towelling gowns – and a magnificent early-Georgian red pine staircase in the entrance hall with 'barley sugar' banisters. You have the choice of two restaurants and there are ten new bedrooms in the old mews and stables. Book early.

~

NEARBY Rock of Cashel; Holycross Abbey; Clonmel.
LOCATION in gardens, set back off road in town centre; parking available
MEALS breakfast, lunch, dinner
PRICES rooms I£65-I£85pp; standard double I£130; breakfast included; lunch I£4-I£7; dinner I£19
ROOMS 23; 13 in house, 10 in mews; 12 double, 7 twin, 4 single; all with bath and shower; all rooms with phone, tv, hairdrier
FACILITIES garden; private path to Rock; terrace
CREDIT CARDS AE, DC, MC, V
CHILDREN welcome **DISABLED** possible; lift **PETS** not accepted
CLOSED 24-27 Dec **PROPRIETORS** Pat and Susan Murphy

Co Wexford

DRINAGH

KILLIANE CASTLE

~ FARMHOUSE ~

Drinagh, Wexford, Co Wexford
TEL 053 58885/58898 **FAX** 053 58885

THOSE WHO HAVE ALREADY found Killiane Castle tend to have that special expression worn by people who have a secret they want to keep to themselves. For this is a remarkable place and farmer's wife, Kathleen Mernagh, a most charming and thoughtful hostess. The Mernaghs' early 18thC house was built inside the walls of a largely intact Norman castle, complete with tower (now listed) and dungeon. From the back rooms, you see the ruins of a small chapel in a field and the marshes running down to the sea. Down a leafy lane, miles from the main road, it seems centuries away from everywhere else. Twice a day, you can hear the hum of machines as the cows file in and out of the milking parlour. Kathleen Mernagh, mother of five boys, loves what she does and she does it extremely well. Long before she married a farmer she worked in hotel management. Our reporter heard one guest say to another at breakfast (Jack Mernagh serves his wife's dishes): "It's just like a small hotel." Some bedrooms overlook the weeping ash at the front of the house; more interesting ones overlook the courtyard and over the castle walls to green countryside beyond. All are spacious, well-equipped and comfortable. Happy birds twitter and swoop over the rooftops of this historic place, only a short drive from Rosslare.

~

NEARBY Wexford; Rosslare; Waterford Harbour; Kilmore Quay.
LOCATION in farmland, 3 miles (5 km) from Wexford; parking available
MEALS breakfast
PRICES rooms I£20pp; standard double I£40; breakfast included
ROOMS 8; 3 double, 2 twin, 2 family; 6 with bath; 2 with shower; all rooms with tv, hairdrier; iron in corridor; tea/coffee making facilities under stairs
FACILITIES garden, terrace; tennis court; public telephone
CREDIT CARDS MC, V
CHILDREN welcome
DISABLED no **PETS** not in house **CLOSED** 1 Dec to 1 Mar
PROPRIETORS Jack and Kathleen Mernagh

Co Wicklow

ENNISKERRY, GLENCREE VALLEY

ENNISCREE LODGE HOTEL
~ COUNTRY HOTEL ~

Enniskerry, Glencree Valley, Co Wicklow
TEL 01 2863542 **FAX** 01 2866037
E-MAIL enniscree@iol.ie

THIS LITTLE CORN-COLOURED HOTEL with slate roof, tucked away in the Wicklow mountains, has an Alpine chalet feel about it and recently started a new life in the enthusiastic hands of hoteliers' son Raymond Power (one of the Powers of nearby Tinakilly) and his wife, Josephine. The air is so fresh, the nights so still and quiet, and the setting in the wooded valley so remote that it is impossible to believe the bustling centre of Dublin is not much more than a half-an-hour's drive away. The small and intimate scale gives the lodge a particular charm of its own. Downstairs rooms are delightfully cosy, with glowing log fires and pine panelling. There is a small beamed bar with window seats, and the dining-room has stunning views of the valley and distant peaks. Outside, there is an enclosed courtyard, with a cherry tree, where, weather permitting, you can have a drink before dinner or sit out late to take the night air. Hardly an obvious conference venue, the lodge has become very sought after for small groups of staff or executives to work on special projects. It is not unusual to see them about; the natural setting seems to provide mental stimulus and relaxation. Eating is taken seriously; when we visited there was a chef specializing in French/Irish cuisine, using local produce such as Wicklow lamb, fish and game.

~

NEARBY Enniskerry village; Powerscourt; Glendalough; Wicklow Way.
LOCATION in garden and grounds, 4 miles (6 km) from Enniskerry; signposted on road to Glencree; parking available
MEALS breakfast, dinner
PRICES rooms I£45pp; standard double I£90; breakfast included; dinner I£30
ROOMS 10; 8 double, 1 twin, 1 single; 4 with bath, 6 with shower; all with phone, tv, tea/ coffee making facilities; hairdrier available
FACILITIES terraces, gardens
CREDIT CARDS all major
CHILDREN welcome **DISABLED** not possible **PETS** not accepted
CLOSED 25 and 26 Dec **PROPRIETORS** Raymond and Josephine Power

Co Wexford

GOREY

MARLFIELD HOUSE
~ COUNTRY HOUSE ~

Courtown Road, Gorey, Co Wexford
TEL 055 21124 **FAX** 055 21572
E-MAIL marlf@iol.ie

A SIGN IN THE DRIVE of this stunning Regency house once owned by the Earls of Courtown and now a Relais and Chateaux hotel (one of the best in Ireland), reads: 'Drive carefully, pheasants crossing'. Not only is this a preserve of all good things for people, but it is pretty comfortable for animals, too. There's a little dog basket for a terrier beside the 18thC marble fireplace in the semi-circular architect-designed hall. Mary Bowe's peacocks, bantams, ducks and geese are cherished and indulged almost as much as her guests. This is a gorgeous, overblown place, a feast for the eyes because of Mary's passion for interior decoration. Her taste is reflected in Waterford crystal chandeliers, little French chairs, gilded taps and a domed conservatory dining-room, with *trompe l'oeil* and trellis. Garlanded with awards – Hostess of the Year, Wine List of the Year, Best Breakfast, One of the World's Most Enchanting Hideaways – the hotel has a tradition of warm hospitality and the Bowes' daughter, Margaret, is now very much at the helm. Bedrooms are sumptuous and charming. Jewels in the crown are the State Rooms, decorated with rich fabrics and fine antique furniture: the French Room, with marble bathroom, overlooks the lake; the Print Room has views of the rose garden. Outstanding food.

~

NEARBY Waterford; Kilkenny; Wexford; Rosslare; beaches.
LOCATION in 35-acre gardens and woodland, 1 mile (1.6 km) out of Gorey on Wexford road; parking available
MEALS breakfast, lunch, dinner
PRICES rooms I£83pp; State rooms from I£135pp; standard double I£166; breakfast included; lunch I£15; dinner I£36
ROOMS 20; 18 double/twin, 2 single; all rooms with bath; all with phone, tv, hairdrier, trouser press, dressing-gown
FACILITIES gardens, terraces; sauna **CREDIT CARDS** all major
CHILDREN welcome; no under-10s in dining-room **DISABLED** possible **PETS** welcome
CLOSED mid-Dec to mid-Jan **PROPRIETORS** Ray and Mary Bowe; Margaret Bowe

Co Kilkenny

Cullintra House

～ COUNTRY HOUSE ～

The Rower, Inistioge, Co Kilkenny
Tel 051 423614
E-mail cullhse@indigo.ie

Patricia Cantlon is known for her long, leisurely, candlelit dinner parties at the 200-year-old ivy-clad farmhouse where she was born. This is not for those with rigid eating habits. When our inspector called, Patricia had several important jobs to do before getting under way in the kitchen: station herself outside the front door with palette and brushes to finish off a painting; race off to the vet with one of her many cats. The day begins when a guest knocks on her door to alert her that people are up and about and waiting for breakfast (could be noon). Her informality and originality have won friends and admirers all over the world. They leave messages in the visitors' book such as 'Great fun'; 'The house, the surroundings, the food, and most of all Patricia, were a magnificent find'.

She has, indeed, created a bewitching retreat. The low-ceilinged house abounds in artistic extras such as the imaginatively-designed rooms in the green-roofed barn, and the conservatory, where Patricia lights banks of candles for pre-dinner drinks. There are log fires, long walks, conversations with cats and foxes, swimming with Patricia in the river. She's a natural hostess, with persuasive powers to make her guests feel they have entered a place that is not quite of this world. It works. (Maeve Binchy's *Circle of Friends* was filmed in Inistioge.)

～

Nearby Kilkenny, 19 miles (31 km); New Ross, 6 miles (10 km); Jerpoint Abbey; Waterford.
Location in wooded countryside, 6 miles (10 km) from New Ross; parking available
Meals breakfast, dinner
Prices rooms I£20-I£25pp; standard double I£40; dinner I£16
Rooms 6; 5 double/twin, 1 family; 2 with bath, 4 with shower; hairdrier available; all rooms equipped with hot water bottle
Facilities gardens, terrace; courtyard **Credit cards** extra charge of 3 per cent
Children welcome **Disabled** not possible
Pets by prior arrangement **Closed** never **Proprietor** Patricia Cantlon

Co Kilkenny

JENKINSTOWN

SWIFT'S HEATH
~ COUNTRY HOUSE ~

Jenkinstown, Co Kilkenny
TEL 056 67653 **FAX** 056 67653

SWIFT'S HEATH is one of Ireland's historic houses, with lovely curved staircase and surrounded by farmland and fields of corn. Brigitte Lennon's guest rooms are often occupied by academics and writers soaking up the atmosphere of a house where, in the late 17thC, the young Jonathan Swift stayed with his uncle while he attended school in Kilkenny, before going on to Trinity College, Dublin. Brigitte is quite used to Japanese professors staring out of the tall windows at the mature trees around the house, trying to transport themselves back in time, and to discussions about Swift's satire, *Gulliver's Travels,* and islands inhabited by tiny Lilliputians, people as tall as steeples, thinking horses and Yahoos. As well as the Swiftians, you might well find rock stars, diplomats, and people coming to stay to ride out with the North Kilkenny Hunt. Brigitte's spotless and comfortable rooms are filled with colour and light; one overlooks the stable yard; another has a roll-top bath in an original bathroom. The place has a natural elegance and character all of its own: built in 1651 by a Swift, it remained in the family until 1970 when it was acquired by the Lennons. Brigitte, who is German and an interior decorator, is a delightful hostess and gives guests a warm welcome to this important and interesting place.

~

NEARBY Rock of Cashel; Waterford; Wexford; Mount Juliet; Kilkenny.
LOCATION in gardens and farmland, 6 miles (10 km) out of Kilkenny on the N77 Ballyragget road; parking available
MEALS breakfast
PRICES rooms I£30pp; standard double I£60; breakfast included
ROOMS 3; 2 double, 1 twin; 1 with bath, 2 with shower; all with hairdrier, hot water bottle, electric blanket
FACILITIES gardens, terraces; grass tennis court; hunting arranged
CREDIT CARDS MC, V
CHILDREN over 12 **DISABLED** no downstairs rooms **PETS** not in rooms
CLOSED 21 Dec to 1 Feb **PROPRIETOR** Brigitte Lennon

CO KILKENNY

BUTLER HOUSE
~ TOWNHOUSE ~

16 Patrick Street, Kilkenny, Co Kilkenny
TEL 056 65707/22828 **FAX** 056 65626
E-MAIL res@butler.ie

T HIS TALL, GRAND GEORGIAN HOUSE was once the dower house to Kilkenny Castle, family seat of the Earls of Ormonde. It has beautiful sweeping staircases, plastered ceilings and marble fireplaces. In the 1970s, the house was refurbished in contemporary style by Kilkenny Design, and the result is stunning. The lovely lines and spaces of the Georgian interior have been enhanced by square, modern furniture and neutral colours in carpets and fabrics in the airy, uncluttered rooms. The designers chose black oak furniture, oatmeal carpets, cream curtains, tweed chair covers and the effect, with acres of white walls, is ordered, quiet and restful. Safely lodged at Butler House, you are right in the middle of Kilkenny, a busy tourist centre, and you have your own path to the castle that leads from the back of the house through the formal walled garden, and former stableyards, now converted to crafts workshops. In the cellar is The Basement Restaurant, (where guests go for breakfast), decorated with black and white photographs, black chairs, and all-white china. Morning coffee, biscuits and cake (all very BH colours) are served on a pale oak table in the entrance hall, which has white columns and heavy cream curtains. Superior bedrooms have bay windows and garden and castle views. Butler House is now run by the Kilkenny Civic Trust.

~

NEARBY Kilkenny Castle; cathedral; Kilkenny Design Centre.
LOCATION in gardens, in centre of town; parking available
MEALS breakfast, lunch, dinner
PRICES rooms I£49.50pp-I£64.50pp; standard double I£99; breakfast included; lunch from I£4.95; dinner I£20
ROOMS 13; 11 double, 2 twin; 1 with bath, 12 with shower; all with phone, tv, radio, hairdrier, trouser press; some rooms have desks
FACILITIES garden, terrace
CREDIT CARDS all major **CHILDREN** welcome
DISABLED not possible **PETS** not accepted **CLOSED** 24-29 Dec
PROPRIETORS Kilkenny Civic Trust **ACTING MANAGER** Gabrielle Hickey

Co Waterford

The Castle Farm

~ FARM GUEST-HOUSE ~

Millstreet, Cappagh, Dungarvan, Co Waterford
TEL 058 68049 **FAX** 68099

REGULARS AT THIS CONVERTED FARMHOUSE, within the keep of a small 15thC castle on a rock among the lush green fields of the Blackwater Valley, know what they like: the Nugents have an 80 per cent repeat business. There is the walk down the drive that was once an avenue of elms, through the imposing front gates and along the lane to the little stone bridge over the River Finisk. The air is heavy with the scent of water and grass, and you may be joined by Bob, the house dog. You might have the bedroom in the original tower known as Miss O'Keeffe's Ballroom (in the 1700s the house belonged to her family). Meals come from Joan Nugent's farmhouse kitchen and are served in the yellow dining-room, with walls more than five-and-half-feet thick and an original 15thC stone archway. Emmett Nugent can nearly always be distracted from his tasks to relate the history of his fascinating edifice. He has made a path around the base of the rocky mound, so visitors may make a circular tour; and he has also restored a clammy dungeon where, he explains, guests like to gather on warm evenings to enjoy a glass or two and get up to some 'medieval' fun and games. Joan also likes to hang her washing there. You feel that somehow you are the first to discover the comforting peace and quiet of Castle Farm. The Nugents are delightful, welcoming and thoughtful hosts.

~

NEARBY Cappoquin, 5 miles (8 km); Dungarvan; Waterford; Youghal.
LOCATION in countryside, on a 120-acre dairy farm, 9 miles (14 km) from Dungarvon; parking available
MEALS breakfast, lunch
PRICES rooms I£23-I£25pp; standard double I£46; dinner I£15-I£17
ROOMS 4; double and single in each room; 1 with bath, 3 with shower; all with tv, hairdrier; tea/coffee making facilities
FACILITIES gardens, terraces
CREDIT CARDS AE, MC, V **CHILDREN** welcome
DISABLED no downstairs rooms **PETS** small dogs, with baskets, accepted
CLOSED 1 Nov to 14 Mar **PROPRIETORS** Joan and Emmett Nugent

Co Wicklow

HUNTER'S HOTEL
~ COACHING INN ~

Newrath Bridge, Rathnew, Co Wicklow
TEL 0404 40106 **FAX** 0404 40338
E-MAIL reception@hunters.ie

THE AREA AROUND IT is fast becoming part of Dublin commuterland, but not many changes here in this little island of constancy. In 1840, some Victorian travellers touring Ireland reported: 'We strongly recommend Mr Hunter's Inn at Newrath Bridge, which is, according to our experience, the most comfortable in the county.' The same applies today. This is a delightful, proudly old-fashioned place, built as a coaching inn for several big houses in the vicinity. You would not be surprised if you were to hear the sound of horses' hooves and carriage wheels clattering into the enormous stable yard, or trunks being carried into the beamed front hall, which still has the tiled floor laid in 1720. Nothing clashes, nothing jars, to spoil the old world charm that brings people from far and wide. Present owner Maureen Gelletlie (a great great granddaughter of the original Mr Hunter) is renowned for her individual style of looking after guests. In a trice she manages to get complete strangers talking in the small bar, with bare, wide wooden floorboards, beams, and a print of the 1900 Grand National winner, Ambush 11, on the wall, where she serves drinks. There is good, plain cooking; a lovely garden by the river; courtesy; glowing fires; charming bedrooms (ask for garden view); tea on the lawn; billowing wisteria.

~

NEARBY Powerscourt Gardens; Russborough House; Glendalough; golf.
LOCATION in gardens on River Varty, in countryside half a mile from Rathnew; parking available
MEALS breakfast, lunch, dinner
PRICES rooms I£52.50pp; standard double I£105; breakfast included; lunch I£15; dinner I£15
ROOMS 16; 15 double/twin, 1 single, 15 with bath, 1 with shower; all rooms with phone, tv, hairdrier; hot water bottle
FACILITIES gardens, terrace
CREDIT CARDS all major **CHILDREN** welcome **DISABLED** ground-floor room
PETS accepted **CLOSED** 24-26 Dec **PROPRIETORS** the Gelletlie family

CO WICKLOW

WICKLOW TOWN

THE OLD RECTORY
~ TOWN GUEST-HOUSE ~

Wicklow Town, Co Wicklow
TEL 0404 67048 FAX 0404 69181
E-MAIL mail@oldrectory.ie

IN HER BIG KITCHEN, Linda Saunders cooks with flowers – sausages of Wicklow lamb with lavender, peppermint meringues filled with fresh strawberries and rosewater cream and decorated with frosted primroses – and she holds cookery courses in floral cuisine. She and her husband, Paul (once a fireman), welcome guests to their rose-pink Victorian rectory, which has, as is the tradition, a white fireplace (in the sitting-room) for happy events and a black one (in the dining-room) for sadder occasions. The house is a riot of flowers, or 'unashamedly floral' as the Saunders would say: they rampage all over wallpapers, curtains, pillowcases; vases of them adorn every room; they decorate the tables in the dining-room; marigold petals, pansies and chive flowers are scattered over supper. It is contrived to be romantic and runs very smoothly. This is a little doll's house, a love nest, with the standard of service you would expect from a hotel. You may have your breakfast (choose from a long menu) in bed; with champagne or Buck's Fizz if you wish. Don't be surprised to find some flowers on the tray. Wicklow is a delightful, historic little town, with fishing boats and yachts in the harbour; Paul and Linda have devised a walking trail taking in points of interest that starts at the back gate of The Old Rectory (map and quite testing quiz provided).

~

NEARBY Parnell birthplace; Brittas Bay; Meeting of the Waters; Avoca.
LOCATION in gardens, on R750 coming in to town from Rathnew
(by Statoil garage); parking available
MEALS breakfast, lunch
PRICES rooms I£52pp; standard double I£104; breakfast included; dinner I£30.50
ROOMS 8; 2 double, 5 double/twin, 1 family; all with bath and shower; all with
phone, tv, radio, hairdrier, trouser press
FACILITIES garden; gym, sauna
CREDIT CARDS all major
CHILDREN welcome DISABLED possible PETS not accepted CLOSED Jan and Feb
PROPRIETORS Linda and Paul Saunders

Co Dublin

Anglesea Town House
~ TOWN HOUSE ~

63 Anglesea Road, Ballsbridge, Dublin 4
TEL 01 668 3877 **FAX** 01 668 3461

BALLSBRIDGE – A LEAFY SUBURB across the Grand Canal from the city centre – is where many of Dublin's best hotels and restaurants are to be found. Helen Kirrane's large Edwardian house near Herbert Park is in a grand terrace and the minute you step into the hall, with its Tiffany lamps and watered silk curtains, you return to unhurried, gracious times. This house operates at its own stately pace, gently sweeping you along. The famed, prize-winning breakfasts are almost ceremonial: served at a Chippendale table on Wedgwood; accompanied by fresh flowers and white napkins folded into roses. One food critic describes them as 'orchestrated and meticulous' – 'gorgeous'. Mrs Kirrane, an ex-teacher, has been welcoming guests for 15 years and finds baking and house-keeping a perfect outlet for her creative talent. One element of the mighty Anglesea breakfast is her baked cereal – a secret recipe – with fruit, apples and nuts, fresh cream and Irish Mist liquor. Those on diets who bewail the numerous courses should, she says, just try to admire how "pretty" the whole show is. Guests are free to wander at will in the house – into the kitchen, too. There's a garden to sit in and an elegant drawing room with Edwardian fireplace, maple floor, books and magazines. Enduring friendships have been made here. Afternoon tea.

NEARBY city centre, 4 miles (6 km); rugby at Landsdowne Road.
LOCATION close to Lansdowne Road rugby ground and short walk from Sandymount Rd DART station; with parking
MEALS breakfast
PRICES rooms I£45pp; standard double I£90; breakfast included
ROOMS 7; 2 with bath,; 5 with shower; all with phone, tv, radio, hairdrier, dressing-gown
FACILITIES drawing-room; garden; ironing service in basement
CREDIT CARDS AE, MC, V
CHILDREN welcome; baby-sitting **DISABLED** not possible **PETS** not accepted
CLOSED 22 Dec to 6 Jan **PROPRIETORS** Helen Kirrane and family

Co Dublin

CENTRAL

BROWNES BRASSERIE AND TOWNHOUSE

~ RESTAURANT WITH ROOMS ~

22 St Stephen's Green, Dublin 2
TEL 01 638 3939 **FAX** 01 638 3900
E-MAIL info@brownesdublin.com

THIS CLASSY NEW B&B is decidedly not in the minimalist mode of the smart new Fitzwilliam (located nearby), more an ode to Georgian Dublin: an elegant, listed townhouse on St Stephen's Green, only a few doors down from the Shelbourne. Owner Barry Canny spent more than I£1m on refurbishing what used to be the clubhouse of The Order of Friendly Brothers of St Patrick, founded in the 18thC to stop duelling. It is sumptuous. Mr Canny sees it as a "country house in the heart of the city"; he and his wife, Dee, shipped in antiques from Paris, London and Barcelona and used some top names in interior design and fabrics. Bathrooms have pink Alicante marble counter tops; bedrooms have fax and ISDN lines and 'laptop capability'. Some are on the smallish side. The classic Georgian exterior is untouched; inside great care has gone into keeping to the style of the building. The drawing-room has an Adam fireplace moved from a floor above and the room's mahogany door has been copied for all the bedrooms. The lift has been discreetly hidden away. An ingenious front suite doubles as an office, with a bed that folds away in the wall to become bookshelves, and a boardroom table that breaks up into smaller tables. The 'brasserie' at street level has been described as a bit 'fin-de-siècle Paris'; house guests have it to themselves for breakfast.

~

NEARBY Grafton Street; Trinity College; Temple Bar.
LOCATION overlooking St Stephen's Green; parking available
MEALS breakfast, lunch, dinner
PRICES rooms I£155 to I£300; standard double I£155; superior double I£165; single I£100 ; breakfast included; lunch I£10; dinner I£25
ROOMS 12; 8 double, 2 twin/double, 1 twin, 1 single; all with bath; all rooms with phone, tv, radio, hairdrier, a/c, ISDN and fax lines; trouser press by request; safe in office **FACILITIES** drawing-room **CREDIT CARDS** all major
CHILDREN welcome **DISABLED** possible **PETS** by arrangement **CLOSED** Christmas Day
PROPRIETOR Barry Canny **MANAGERS** Ronan and Anne Branigan

Co Dublin

CENTRAL

KILRONAN HOUSE

~ TOWN GUEST-HOUSE ~

70 Adelaide Road, Dublin 2
TEL 01 475 5266/5266 **FAX** 01 478 2841

THIS VETERAN, reasonably-priced Georgian guest-house in a quiet, leafy, residential street near St Stephen's Green has been in business for more than 30 years and is perfectly situated for walking to some of the city's most famous landmarks and shops. A new owner has just taken over and may carry out improvements, though there had been overhauls under the previous proprietors. Our reporter felt the exterior could do with a lick of paint but, once inside, was impressed with the warm, yellow walls and parquet floor of the entrance hall and the welcoming reception area tucked under the stairs. Bedrooms are on four 'creaking' floors, and it is a long climb to the top. Some are on the small side. Colours tend to be yellow again, with elegant fabrics and pretty, white-painted wrought-iron bedheads, some pine furniture, heavy off-white curtains and the odd print on the walls. We were told of one room – below ground level – that was described as 'tiny', so it is clearly advisable to check in advance which rooms are available. The yellow sitting-room has a big, gilt-edged mirror over the fireplace, antique furniture and a chandelier. The yellow extends to the breakfast-room, with shining silver and crisp white linens on the tables. The overall feel of the place is old-fashioned, comfortable and relaxed. Reports, please.

~

NEARBY Grafton Street; National Gallery; Trinity College.
LOCATION 5 minutes walk S of St Stephen's Green; private, secure parking available
MEALS breakfast
PRICES rooms I£30-I£47.50pp; standard double I£90; single I£55; breakfast included
ROOMS 15; 11 double (8 twin), 2 single, 2 family; all with shower; all with phone, tv, hairdrier; safe in reception
FACILITIES sitting-room **CREDIT CARDS** all major **CHILDREN** over 10
DISABLED 1 room 4 steps down; no special facilities **PETS** not accepted
CLOSED never **PROPRIETOR** Terry Masterson

CO DUBLIN

CENTRAL

NUMBER 31

~ TOWN GUEST-HOUSE ~

31 Leeson Close, Dublin 2
TEL 01 676 5011 **FAX** 01 676 2929
E-MAIL number31@iol.ie

HOMER, THE YELLOW LABRADOR who was very much part of the household at Kilronan House (page 122), has settled well into his new home at Number 31, which has been taken over by his owners, delightful hosts Noel and Deirdre Comer. This is a very special and visually pleasing place: a mews house designed in the mid-1960s by controversial Dublin architect, Sam Stephenson, and the Georgian house across the garden that was acquired three years ago giving much more space. The Comers loved the originality from the outset and do not plan to make major changes. Only a plate on the wall with '31' on it indicates this is somewhere you may stay. The Stephenson building is modern and open-plan, with painted white brickwork and much glass, wood and stone; kilims hang on the wall. There's a little sunken sitting area, with a black leather sofa custom-built around the fire. French windows and wooden decking lead to the garden and the back of the Georgian house. Deirdre's generous and delicious breakfasts (home-made breads, jams, potato cakes, granola) are served in a white upstairs room on long tables with fresh flowers, sparkling silver, and white linen napkins. Five stylish bedrooms are in the mews house (two have patios). Fifteen more are in the Georgian house, with moulded ceilings and painted in National Trust colours.

~

NEARBY St Stephen's Green; National Gallery; Grafton Street.
LOCATION just off Lower Leeson Street; 5 minutes walk from St Stephen's Green; parking available **MEALS** breakfast
PRICES rooms I£47pp-I£55pp; standard double I£94; breakfast included
ROOMS 20; 15 double (12 twin), 5 family; 17 with bath, 3 with shower; all with phone, tv, hairdrier; safe at reception
FACILITIES garden; sitting-room, breakfast-room, conservatory
CREDIT CARDS all major **CHILDREN** over 10 **DISABLED** 2 ground-floor rooms
PETS small dogs accepted; not in breakfast-room **CLOSED** never
PROPRIETORS Noel and Deirdre Comer

CO DUBLIN

CENTRAL

TRINITY LODGE
～ TOWNHOUSE ～

12 South Frederick Street, Dublin 2
TEL 01 679 5044/5184 **FAX** 01 679 5223
E-MAIL trinitylodge@tinet.ie

OWNER PETER MURPHY opened this three-storey Georgian house in the heart of Dublin just off Nassau Street opposite Trinity College – in 1997 as an elegant, little guest-house that would not have any of the things he hates about hotels. So, guests are given individual attention from the moment they step in through the blue front door and he places a candle in each room to give a special romantic glow to evenings. This is a handsome, listed building and in order to keep its character and symmetry, Peter chose not to put in a lift, or carve chunks out of rooms for bathrooms. But, he's got almost everything else in the way of comfort and convenience, such as air-conditioning, trouser presses and personal safes. Colours are appropriately Georgian, green, deep red, yellow. There's a little sitting area in the entrance hall, with a window looking on to the street and some comfortable armchairs. Pictures in the house are by the Dublin artist, Graham Knuttel, who lives next door and whose work is very popular with Hollywood stars (he has a commission to paint a portrait for Robert de Niro). They are in bold bright colours and, as one of the staff observes, "have very suspicious-looking people in them, who don't want to look directly at you". You can walk easily to all the local sights from here.

～

NEARBY National Art Gallery; Temple Bar; Dublin Castle; the Liffey.
LOCATION a short walk from Trinity College; limited parking available (with charge; booking essential)
MEALS breakfast
PRICES rooms standard double I£95; superior double I£120; single I£60; breakfast included
ROOMS 13; 2 double, 2 single, 6 family (with twin beds), 3 suites with lounge and kitchen area; all with shower; all rooms with phone, tv, radio, hairdrier, trouser press, air-conditioning, safe
FACILITIES sitting-room
CREDIT CARDS AE, MC, V **CHILDREN** welcome **DISABLED** not possible
PETS not accepted **CLOSED** never **PROPRIETOR** Peter Murphy

Co Kildare

Leixlip

Leixlip House Hotel

~ VILLAGE HOTEL ~

Captain's Hill, Leixlip, Co Kildare
Tel 01 624 2268 **Fax** 01 624 4177
E-MAIL manager@lvhh.iol.ie

L EIXLIP IS A PRETTY VILLAGE on the Liffey with interesting, old houses behind high walls and a main street of little shops. It is not quite as rural as it once was, being so near to Dublin and bang in the middle of what could be called Silicon Valley, but it hangs on to its charm all the same. This flat-fronted Georgian house was built in 1772 for a Captain Brady who commanded a small garrison in Leixlip. Its fine gates and pillars were brought from Frenchpark in Co Roscommon. Rebuilt and refurbished after a fire in 1984, it is now a comfortable, smart little 'boutique' hotel, with an acclaimed restaurant, much frequented by Dubliners. Standards are kept high because many of the regular clientele are American executives connected with the nearby big IT companies, and so you get all kinds of indulgences like shaving mirrors, bathrobes, plenty of toiletries in the bathroom, chocolates and extra towels put out for you at night. Like all pleasant, old-fashioned hotels, you put your shoes outside your door before you go to bed and there they are in the morning, cleaned and polished. By special arrangement, you may use the gym, steam room and sauna over the road and the video shop, too. The young manager, Christian Schmelter, worked at one of the best hotels in Ireland, Sheen Falls Lodge, and likes nothing more than to spoil his guests. Room service, of course.

~

Nearby Dublin city centre, 8 miles (13 km); Dublin airport.
Location in village; ample parking
Meals breakfast, lunch, dinner
Prices rooms I£60-I£70pp; standard double I£120; single I£90/I£110; breakfast included; lunch I£14; dinner I£25
Rooms 15; 12 double, 2 twin, 1 single; all with bath and shower; all rooms with phone, tv, radio, hairdrier; trouser press
Facilities sitting-room, restaurant; terrace under beech tree **Credit cards** all major **Children** welcome **Disabled** not possible **Pets** not accepted
Closed Christmas Day **Proprietor** Frank Towey **Manager** Christian Schmelter

Co Kildare

MOYGLARE MANOR
~ COUNTRY HOUSE ~

Moyglare, Maynooth, Co Kildare
TEL 01 6286351 **FAX** 01 6285405
E-MAIL moyglaremanor@iol.ie

THIS LOVELY 18THC stone country house in the middle of the stud farm belt is so opulent as to seem fabulously decadent. When we visited, people were having *lunch* by candlelight in the gorgeous deep pink, chandeliered dining-room, with draped curtains as thick as blankets, blazing fires and potted palms. A sweet aroma of roses comes in from the garden, filled with tall, dignified trees, and clouds of clematis cover the back of the house. Our inspector had never seen quite so many varieties of decorated lampshade: pleated, tasselled, fringed; or so many fabulous arrangements of flowers. It is all very Naughty Nineties, with lashings of Regency stripes, alabaster vases, and rooms crammed with ornate antique furniture, square chairs, round chairs, stuffed and buttoned chairs, and heavy gilt mirrors, put together so artfully by owner Nora Devlin to make a world of its own. It is meant to be fun – and it is. Bedrooms are large and comfortable, some with love seats, four-posters, and lashings of pink, ribbons and bows, drapes and frills. The history of the house is long and fascinating: Bridget, Countess of Tyrconnell, heard of the Flight of the Earls while walking in the garden here in 1607. The award-winning 16-page wine list is also long and fascinating; in the cellar is almost every Chateau Yquem since 1945.

~

NEARBY Maynooth; horses; Castletown House; National Stud.
LOCATION in gardens in countryside, 3 miles (5 km) from Maynooth; parking available
MEALS breakfast, lunch, dinner
PRICES rooms I£75pp; standard double I£150; breakfast included; lunch from I£15; dinner I£26.95
ROOMS 16; 14 double/twin, 2 triples; all with bath; all with phone, radio, hairdrier; some with trouser press; tv on request; all with tea/coffee making facilities
FACILITIES gardens, terraces
CREDIT CARDS all major **CHILDREN** over 12 **DISABLED** possible **PETS** not accepted
CLOSED 24-26 Dec **PROPRIETOR** Norah Devlin **MANAGER** Shay Curran

Co Laois

MOUNTRATH

ROUNDWOOD HOUSE
~ COUNTRY HOUSE ~

Mountrath, Co Laois
TEL 0502 32120 **FAX** 0502 32711

A RECENT REPORTER REACTED very well to the Kennans' operation. The house is 'not in perfect repair, but for the type of place they run, this didn't seem to matter': it's a 'wonderful place, and the Kennans really are charming and informal hosts'.

The perfectly proportioned Palladian mansion is set in acres of lime, beech and chestnut woodland. The Kennans have wholeheartedly continued the work of the Irish Georgian Society, who rescued the house from near-ruin in the 1970s. All the Georgian trappings remain – bold paintwork, shutters instead of curtains, rugs instead of fitted carpets, and emphatically no TV. Despite this, the house is decidedly lived in, certainly not a museum.

For Rosemarie's plentiful meals, non-residents sit at separate tables; residents must sit together – you don't have a choice – fine if you like to chat to strangers, not ideal for romantic twosomes. After-dinner conversation is also encouraged over coffee and drinks by the open fire in the drawing-room. You may well find the Kennans joining in.

Four pleasant extra bedrooms in a recently converted stable block are perhaps cosier and of a better standard than those in the main house. It's very child-friendly (the Kennans have six), with a lovely big playroom at the top of the house, full of toys.

~

NEARBY walking, horse-riding, fishing; Slieve Bloom mountains.
LOCATION in countryside, 3 miles (5 km) N of Mountrath on Kinnitty road; with gardens and ample car parking
MEALS full breakfast, lunch on Sunday only, dinner; wine licence
PRICES B&B I£41-I£51; Sunday lunch I£12; dinner I£23
ROOMS 9; 7 double (3 twin), 2 family rooms; all with bath; all rooms have central heating **FACILITIES** sitting-room, study, dining-room, hall; croquet
CREDIT CARDS AE, DC, MC, V **CHILDREN** very welcome **DISABLED** not suitable
PETS accepted by arrangement **CLOSED** Christmas Day
PROPRIETORS Frank and Rosemarie Kennan

Co Roscommon

GLEESON'S RESTAURANT AND GUESTHOUSE

~ TOWN GUEST-HOUSE ~

Market Square, Roscommon, Co Roscommon
TEL 0903 29654 **FAX** 27425
E-MAIL gleerest@iol.ie

ROSCOMMON IS AN ATTRACTIVE, bustling little town with some handsome stone buildings, including a former courthouse and county jail. Way off the tourist circuit, it is surrounded by green pastures filled with sheep and cattle. Mary and Eamon Gleeson were primary school teachers when they decided to sell everything they had to buy a derelict 19thC manse in the market square, which they have converted into a homely, friendly place that is very much part of local life. There's a constant stream of people calling in to eat in the restaurant or to read a paper or meet friends in the coffee shop. It's most agreeable and interesting to be in the middle of such activity as Mary Gleeson, in her chef's 'whites', dashes in and out of the kitchen with trays of freshly-baked scones and cakes for the coffee shop – with fire, original floorboards and exposed stone walls – and organizes the day's menu in the restaurant. Upstairs, rooms are smart, smallish and comfortable; Mary has put good quality beds and showers on top of her list of priorities. Some standard rooms have plain wooden floors. When we visited she was in the process of turning one room into a small library for guests. Outside is a paved forecourt with trees, where you can sit with a cup of coffee and watch the world go by. The Tourist Office is, handily, next door.

~

NEARBY Roscommon Abbey; Roscommon Castle.
LOCATION in town centre; parking available
MEALS breakfast, lunch, dinner
PRICES rooms I£25pp; standard double I£50; suite I£95; breakfast included; lunch I£5; dinner I£10-I£12
ROOMS 20: 15 double/twin, 4 single, 1 executive suite with hydrotherapy bath; all with bath/shower; all rooms with phone, tv, radio, hairdrier, trouser press, tea/coffee making facilities
FACILITIES restaurant; coffee shop; terrace **CREDIT CARDS** AE, MC, V
CHILDREN welcome **DISABLED** not possible **PETS** not possible
CLOSED 25 and 26 Dec **PROPRIETORS** Mary and Eamon Gleeson

Co Down/Co Antrim

Glassdrumman Lodge

~ COUNTRY HOUSE AND RESTAURANT ~

85 Mill Road, Annalong, Co Down BT34 4RH
Tel 028 4376 8585/8451 **Fax** 028 4376 7041

OUR REPORTER LOVED the 'fantastic' position of this family-run, friendly country house: 'nestling in the foothills of the Mourne Mountains, with sea on one side, mountains on the other'. Stone walls surround well-kept gardens and there are old stable blocks. Graeme and Joan Hall believe in 'simple excellence'. All bedrooms have modern comforts and good views. This is ideal walking country, and many guests are golfers who have come to play on the nearby Royal County Down course. Breakfast is served on a long table; dinner, too, though small tables are available. The restaurant has an excellent reputation: sausages are home-made and fresh seasonal dishes come with home-grown herbs and vegetables.

~

Nearby golf at Royal County Down, 7 miles (11 km); beaches, 1 mile (1.5 km).
Location in garden and grounds, 7 miles (11 km) S of Newcastle on A2, 1 mile (1.6 km) W of Annalong; ample parking **Meals** breakfast, dinner
Prices rooms £90 (single) to £140; standard double £110; breakfast included; dinner £32.50 **Rooms** 10; 8 double/twin, 2 suites; all with bath/shower; all rooms with phone, tv; safe in reception **Facilities** gardens, terraces **Credit cards** all major **Children** accepted **Disabled** downstairs suite and ramps **Pets** not inside; kennels **Closed** never **Proprietors** the Hall family

Galgorm Manor

~ MANOR HOUSE HOTEL ~

136 Fenaghy Road, Ballymena, Co Antrim BT42 IEA
Tel 01266 881001 **Fax** 01266 880080

CLASSICAL MUSIC GREETS YOU at this impressive, listed, late 19thC country house that was once the home of a prosperous linen family. It looks over rolling countryside and has its own trout and salmon stream. Many of the bedrooms have views of the river and you can hear the sound of waterfalls. The style is grand and sumptuous: thick carpets, huge flower arrangements, dark mahogany antiques and swathes of fabric in sober colours. More fun is the Gillies Irish pub, with rough stone walls, open fires, wood floor, bar food, and live music twice a week. The manor stands in an 86-acre estate: pleasant walks from the front door. Popular for wedding receptions. Leisure centre planned for 2000.

~

Nearby golf at Royal Portrush, 25 miles (40 km); Giant's Causeway; Bushmills.
Location 4 miles (6 km) W of Ballymena, in extensive grounds; parking available **Meals** breakfast, lunch, dinner
Prices per room £99–£140; standard double £119; breakfast included; lunch £15; dinner £25.50 **Rooms** 24 (plus cottages); 20 double (12 twin), 4 suites; all with bath and shower; all rooms with phone, tv, radio, hairdrier, trouser press; safe in reception **Facilities** gardens, terrace; equestrian centre, fishing, clay pigeon shooting **Credit cards** all major **Children** accepted **Disabled** ground-floor rooms **Pets** not accepted **Closed** never **Manager** David Cadwallader

Co Antrim/Co Down

Londonderry Arms Hotel

~ Seaside hotel ~

20 Harbour Road, Carnlough, Co Antrim BT44 0EU
Tel 028 2888 5255 **Fax** 028 2888 5263 **E-mail** lda@glensofantrim.com

A FAMILY-RUN, ivy-covered hotel which derives much of its appeal from Carnlough's seaside setting – with a little white limestone harbour and big, sandy bay. Traditional, comfortable, reliable, immaculate, it was built in 1848 by the Marchioness of Londonderry as a coaching inn. Some bedrooms – green and Bordeaux colour scheme – overlook the sea; and there's also a delightful seaside garden. The restaurant serves fresh seafood and lamb from the Antrim hills. Public rooms have open log fires, paintings by Ulster artists, and are decorated with bits of driftwood. The Arkle Bar has a collection of memorabilia of the great Irish steeplechaser and a wide range of malt whiskeys.

~

Nearby Glens of Antrim, 5 miles (8 km); Giant's Causeway, 30 miles (48 km); Belfast 40 miles (64 km).
Location in centre of town, across the road from sea front; parking available
Meals breakfast, lunch, dinner **Prices** rooms, £80–£90 double; £48 single; breakfast included; lunch £12.95; dinner £18.95 **Rooms** 35; 29 double (6 twin), 6 family; all with bath and shower; all rooms with phone, tv, radio, hairdrier; safe in reception
Facilities bar, restaurant, sitting-rooms; garden; lift **Credit cards** all major
Children accepted **Disabled** 1 room and lift for access **Pets** not accepted
Closed Christmas Day **Proprietor** Frank O'Neill

The Old Inn

~ Village inn ~

Crawfordsburn, Co Down BT19 IJH
Tel 028 9185 3255 **Fax** 028 9185 2775 **E-mail** info@theoldinn.com

THIS HALF-TIMBERED, partly thatched inn on the main street of a pretty village is said to be the oldest in Ireland, with records going back to 1614, and was used by mail coaches and smugglers. It is best described as quaint on the outside, and inside, too. Plenty of beams and wood panelling, as befitting an inn. But it is undoubtedly very comfortable, with well-equipped bathrooms and smallish bedrooms. Bedcovers and curtains are in dark fabrics; there are carved bedheads and dark parquet floors. Staff wear tartan uniforms. It's a popular choice for wedding receptions and can be very crowded at weekends. Open fires in public rooms; a charming cottage in the garden; two restaurants.

~

Nearby Mount Stewart; Belfast; Bangor; Holywood.
Location on main street, in centre of village; with garden; parking available
Meals breakfast, lunch, dinner
Prices per room £65-£150; standard double £85; breakfast included; lunch £15; dinner £23
Rooms 33; 29 double (2 twin), 2 single, 1 family; 32 with bath and shower, 1 with shower; all rooms with phone, tv, radio, hairdrier, trouser press; safe in reception
Facilities terrace, gardens; bar, restaurants
Credit cards all major **Children** accepted **Disabled** ground-floor rooms
Pets not accepted **Closed** Christmas **General manager** Brendan McCann

Co Fermanagh/Co 'derry

Kesh

Ardess House

~ Country guest-house ~

Kesh, Co Fermanagh
Tel/Fax 028 6863 1267 **E-mail** ardess@clara.net
Website www.fermanaghcraft.com/ardesscraft

DOROTHY PENDRY, who used to teach geography in Belfast, and her husband, Brian, restored this late 18thC rectory near Lough Erne, much of it with their own hands. Dorothy runs a craft centre, with courses in painting, pottery, spinning, weaving, cookery and patchwork. There are peacocks in the gardens and Jacob sheep in the paddock. It is very relaxed, with some lovely furniture – and faded carpets. Breakfast is served in the kitchen – with Aga – and dinner in the red dining-room; organic produce comes from the kitchen garden. Some bedrooms are spacious. One has a collection of ancient, worn teddy bears. Two black labradors and various cats complete the household. Expect to muck in.

~

Nearby walking; fishing; Lough Erne; Castle Coole; Belleek pottery.
Location in countryside, on A32 between Enniskillen and Omagh; parking available
Meals breakfast, dinner
Prices rooms £22.50pp; breakfast included; £35 per person, breakfast and dinner included **Rooms** 4; 2 double/twin, 2 triple; all with bath; all rooms with radio
Facilities garden; craft centre **Credit cards** AE, MC, V **Children** accepted
Disabled not suitable **Pets** not accepted **Closed** Christmas **Proprietor** Dorothy Pendry

Londonderry

Beech Hill Country House Hotel

~ Country hotel ~

32 Ardmore Road, Londonderry, Co Londonderry BT47 3QP
Tel 028 71349 279 **Fax** 028 71345 366 **E-mail** info@beech.hill.com

A STONE GATE LODGE STANDS at the top of the drive leading past lawns, trees, rhododendrons and a small lake to this elegant pale pink house, built in 1729 for a family of English settlers. The comfortable interior has thick carpets and brass chandeliers. The award-winning Ardmore restaurant (the chef is ex-Aubergine/Gordon Ramsey-trained) has formal white linen and gleaming crystal and silver; food is sophisticated 'modern Irish'. Morning room and library have antique furniture and open fires. Bedrooms in the main part of the house are reached by an old staircase with polished banisters; bathrooms are large and well-equipped. A new extension has modern bedrooms and leisure centre.

~

Nearby Giant's Causeway, 20 miles (32 km); Bushmills Distillery; Donegal, 20 miles (32 km).**Location** in gardens and grounds in quiet suburb of Londonderry, 2½ miles (4 km) SE of city centre; parking available **Meals** breakfast, lunch, dinner
Prices per room £69.50-£150; standard double £89.50; breakfast included; lunch £16; dinner £25 **Rooms** 27; 21 double (15 twin), 6 suites; all with bath and shower; all with phone, tv, hairdrier, trouser press; safe on request; modems in suites
Facilities garden; tennis court; sauna; steam room; fitness centre; spa bath; lift
Credit cards all major **Children** accepted **Disabled** 2 rooms and lift **Pets** not accepted **Closed** Christmas Day **Proprietor** Seamus Donnelly

Co Down/Co Donegal

PORTAFERRY HOTEL

~ WATERFRONT INN ~

The Strand, Portaferry, Co Down BT22 IPE
TEL 012477 28231 FAX 012477 28999
048421/

THERE'S A FERRY ACROSS Strangford Lough to this delightful fishing village, which has an unusual aquarium attraction called Exploris. The waterfront is whitewashed, with bright window boxes, and stands on the quayside overlooking the narrow channel connecting the lough with the sea. It is part of a mid-18thC terrace – small, charming and quiet. In the award-winning restaurant, chef John Herlihy has a special way with local seafood and uses the best of Ulster beef, lamb from the Mourne mountains and game from neighbouring estates. Book one of the much sought-after, comfortable, restful bedrooms with views over the gently moving waters of the lough; friendly, attentive staff.

~

NEARBY Mount Stewart; Castle Ward; golf at Royal County Down.
LOCATION on waterfront in Portaferry, on the A2, 29 miles (47 km) SE of Belfast; street parking
MEALS breakfast, lunch, dinner
PRICES rooms £45pp; single £55; standard double £90; breakfast included; lunch £10; dinner £21 **ROOMS** 14; 14 double (5 twin); all with bath; all with phone, tv, radio, hairdrier **FACILITIES** restaurant, bar
CREDIT CARDS all major **CHILDREN** accepted **DISABLED** not suitable **PETS** not accepted
CLOSED Christmas Day **PROPRIETORS** John and Marie Herlihy

FORT ROYAL

~ COUNTRY HOUSE HOTEL ~

Rathmullan, Co Donegal
TEL 074 58100 FAX 074 58103 E-MAIL fortroyal@tinet.ie

THIS WHITE HOUSE, built in 1819, with a number of later additions and converted outbuildings, has been in the Fletcher family since 1948; Robin and Ann Fletcher are welcoming hosts and their son, Tim, is an accomplished cook, who uses herbs, vegetables and soft fruits from the kitchen garden. A previous owner, an ex-Indian Army officer, filled the house with tiger skins; now it is attractively furnished in a more conventional style, with good-sized, comfortable bedrooms, some with views over Lough Swilly. The real treat here is walking down through the gardens to the sandy beach. All is orderly and quiet here, but the 'holiday cottages' in Rathmullan are not appealing.

~

NEARBY Glenveagh National Park; Glebe House; Letterkenny, 15 miles (24 km).
LOCATION in gardens and woodland, on edge of Lough Swilly, on outskirts of village; with parking **MEALS** breakfast, lunch, dinner **PRICES** rooms I£45-I£55pp; standard double I£110; breakfast included; bar lunch from I£5; dinner I£22
ROOMS 15; 4 double, 8 twin, 2 family, 1 single; all with bath/shower; all rooms with phone, tv **FACILITIES** tennis court, 9-hole golf course, public beach
CREDIT CARDS all major **CHILDREN** welcome; high tea provided; no under-10s in dining-room at night **DISABLED** not possible **PETS** welcome with own bedding
CLOSED end Oct to just before Easter **PROPRIETORS** the Fletcher family

Co Donegal

RATHMULLAN, Co DONEGAL

THE WATER'S EDGE

~ WATERSIDE RESTAURANT WITH ROOMS ~

The Ballyboe, Rathmullan, Co Donegal
TEL 074 58182

O N THE SUNNY MORNING we visited this charming little white converted cottage, a rainbow was in the sky over Inch Island and a heron was poking about in the rocks on the edge of the lake. Orla Blaney, a young teacher and one of a large, local family that owns numerous bars and restaurants, had just taken over. Ten of the bedrooms look over water and there is a delightful small, beamed restaurant with simple wooden tables and big picture windows with views of lough and herons. On the menu are local seafood and dishes such as roasted lamb fillet with sweet garlic and rosemary. Newly-painted rooms are basic and bright; new ones in the basement have wooden floors. Cosy TV room. A gem.

~

NEARBY Letterkenny, 12 miles (19 km); Glenveagh National Park; Fanad Head.
LOCATION on the western shore of Lough Swilly, on coast road just before Rathmullan; with parking **MEALS** breakfast, lunch, dinner **PRICES** rooms I£20pp; standard double I£40; I£5 single; breakfast included; lunch from I£8; dinner from I£20 **ROOMS** 13; 9 double, 3 twin, 1 family; 1 with bath, 12 with shower; all rooms with tv, radio; hairdrier available **FACILITIES** restaurant; sitting-room; terrace overlooking water, small garden **CREDIT CARDS** MC, V **CHILDREN** welcomed
DISABLED not possible **PETS** not accepted **CLOSED** never **PROPRIETOR** Orla Blaney

Co Mayo/Co Clare

Belleek Castle

~ Castle hotel ~

Ballina, Co Mayo
Tel 096 22400/21878 **Fax** 096 71750

P URE GOTHIC: not charming at all. Or small. But this late 19thC Scottish baronial 'castle' is so extraordinary it could not be left out. The winding drive, entered through a tall, castellated gateway, passes a huge, new Coca Cola factory. Owner Marshall Doran collects things: the bar is made of timbers from Spanish Armada wrecks; there are suits of jousting armour and giant ammonites in the vaults. The place is filled with red velvet hangings, candles, flagged floors. Jack, the German pointer, has his own sofa on the top landing. But it also has comfortable bedrooms and serves a reasonably straightforward breakfast. Dinner could verge on the medieval.

~

Nearby Westport; Leenane; Lough Conn; fishing; golf.
Location in wooded grounds, 2 miles (3 km) from town centre; ample parking
Meals breakfast; dinner
Prices rooms I£38.50pp-I£71.50pp; standard double I£77; breakfast included; dinner I£25
Rooms 16; 8 double, 1 twin, 4 double four-poster, 1 twin four-poster, 1 family, 1 single; all with bath/shower; all rooms with phone, hairdrier; tv on request
Facilities terraces, garden; bar **Credit cards** AE, MC, V **Children** not suitable
Disabled not suitable **Pets** no dogs in hotel **Closed** 24-26 Dec
Proprietors Jacqueline and Marshall Doran

Gregans Castle

~ Country house hotel ~

Ballyvaughan, Co Clare
Tel 065 77005 **Fax** 065 77111

W E INSPECTED IN 1996 and were impressed with every aspect of Peter and Moira Haden's impeccable and civilized hotel. Bedrooms range from relatively simple to distinctly sumptuous, with lots of space and fine views of the Burren mountains and Galway bay. Pictures of local flora adorn the walls of the cosy, book-filled sitting-room; armchairs, antiques and an open fireplace grace the central hall. The dining-room, with fine views of Galway Bay, has been elegantly and subtly extended; the food is adventurous and satisfying.

~

Nearby The Burren; Cliffs of Moher, 14 miles (22 km).
Location 3½ miles (6 km) south of Ballyvaughan, on N67, in open countryside; in large gardens, with ample car parking
Meals full breakfast, lunch, dinner; full licence
Prices B&B I£49-I£95; DB&B I£83-I£129; reduced rates for longer stays
Rooms 22; 18 double, all with bath, 4 suites with bath and sitting-room; all rooms have central heating, hairdrier
Facilities 2 sitting-rooms (one with TV), bar, dining-room
Credit cards MC, V
Children accepted
Disabled access easy – 7 ground-floor rooms **Pets** not accepted
Closed Nov to Feb **Proprietors** Peter, Moira and Simon-Peter Haden

Co Clare/Co Galway

Hyland's Hotel

~ Village inn ~

Ballyvaughan, Co Clare
Tel 065 77037 **Fax** 065 77131 **E-mail** hylands@tinet.ie

BALLYVAUGHAN IS A DELIGHTFUL little seaside village surrounded by the strange, grey, fissured limestone landscape of the Burren, which becomes a rock garden filled with wild flowers in the spring. This former coaching inn, dating back to the early 18thC and now painted a jolly red and yellow, is owned and run by a seventh and eighth generation of Hylands and is a lively, busy place. Bedrooms have pine furniture; request a newer room at the back for a Burren view and a quieter night. The dining-room with red tablecloths serves delicious local seafood and can get quite crowded when the visitors pour in. Live music in the bar most nights of the week, Irish storytelling less often.

~

Nearby Cliffs of Moher; Aran Islands; Galway City; Coole Park.
Location in seaside village; with parking
Meals breakfast, lunch, dinner
Prices rooms I£38.75pp-I£47pp; standard double I£77.50/I£94; breakfast included; lunch from I£7; dinner from I£18
Rooms 30; double, twin, triple, single; all with bath/shower; all rooms with phone, tv, hairdrier; tea/coffee making facilities **Facilities** restaurant, bar
Credit cards all major **Children** welcome **Disabled** possible **Pets** not accepted
Closed early Jan to Mar **Proprietor** Mary Hyland-Greene

Cashel House

~ Country house hotel ~

Cashel, Connemara, Co Galway
Tel 095 31001 **Fax** 095 31077

DESPITE ITS SIZE, this immaculate white-painted Victorian establishment, with its own beach and set in 50 acres of luxuriant and exotic gardens on the southern finger of Connemara, has the feel of a comfortable and relaxed country house. The antique-laden sitting-rooms are notably cosy, the greatly extended dining-room has been redecorated and the bar is entirely done out in leather. Some of the bedrooms are quite palatial. Food is based on fresh, local ingredients – lobsters, clams, scallops and Connemara lamb.

~

Nearby Kylemore Abbey, 2I miles (35 km); Clifden, 12 miles (19 km); Lough Corrib; Connemara National Park.
Location 42 miles (67 km) W of Galway, 3 miles (5 km) S off N59; ample car parking
Meals breakfast, snack lunch, dinner; full licence
Prices B&B IR£54-IR£80; dinner IR£32-IR£34 (12.5% service charge)
Rooms 32; 16 double, 3 single, I3 mini-suites; all with bath and shower; all have central heating, phone, hairdrier, tv
Facilities 2 sitting-rooms, TV room, library, bar, dining-room; tennis, boat, horse-riding **Credit cards** AE, DC, MC, V **Children** over 5 **Disabled** access easy; several ground-floor bedrooms **Pets** not accepted in public rooms **Closed** 4 Jan to 4 Feb
Proprietors Dermot and Kay McEvilly

Co Galway

ACTONS

~ SEASIDE GUEST-HOUSE AND RESTAURANT ~

Leegaun, Claddaghduff, Co. Galway
TEL 095 44339 FAX 095 44309

THE BUILDING IS A MODERN one: long, white-walled, grey-roofed, in a stunning setting overlooking its own private beach, with nothing in front of it except for grass, sand, sea and sky. Readers have told us of the warm welcome they have received here from owners Rita and Martin Acton, of the high standards of house-keeping and the comfort of the bedrooms. These are fairly plain, with modern furnishings and pretty bedspreads. The dining-room is set in the large central bay of the house, with sea views through windows on three sides. Fish and seafood is the speciality; excellent puddings.

~

NEARBY Clifden; Connemara National Park; Kylemore Abbey.
LOCATION on N59 Galway to Clifden road; in 15 acres of private land, with ample parking
MEALS breakfast, picnic lunch on request, dinner; full licence
PRICES B&B I£25-I£30; special rates for one week's stay; à la carte dinner from I£20
ROOMS 6 double, 3 with bath, 3 with shower; all rooms have phone, tv, tea/coffee kit, hairdrier
FACILITIES 2 sitting-rooms, dining-room; private beach **CREDIT CARDS** AE, DC, MC, V
CHILDREN welcome **DISABLED** all bedrooms on ground floor
PETS not accepted **CLOSED** Nov to mid-Mar **PROPRIETORS** Martin and Rita Acton

ST CLERAN'S

~ COUNTRY HOUSE ~

Craughwell, Co Galway
TEL 091 846555 FAX 092 846600 E-MAIL stcleran@iol.ie

FILM DIRECTOR JOHN HUSTON first saw this limestone Georgian house – 'one of the most beautiful in all Ireland', he said – when out hunting with the Galway Blazers. He bought it, spent a small fortune on restoration, and lived there until 1971. It is now owned by American entertainer, Merv Griffin, who, they say, spent another £2 million. It is very comfortable, with art treasures, antiques, fabrics in bold, contemporary colours, thick Irish carpets, Huston memorabilia – and it is fun. The chef is Japanese; you eat in Huston's old dining-room, possibly where Marlon Brando sat. Prices need not break the bank. There's a charming all-pink bedroom for a one-night indulgence. Excellent service; friendly staff.

~

NEARBY Galway (20 miles (32 km); Connemara; The Burren; golf.
LOCATION in gardens and grounds, 4 miles (6 km) from Craughwell; ample parking
MEALS breakfast; dinner
PRICES rooms I£65-I£125pp; standard double I£130-I£160; breakfast included; dinner I£30.
ROOMS 12; 10 double, 2 twin; 2 with extra bed; all with bath; all rooms with phone, tv, radio, hairdrier, CD player, video, dressing-gown, hot water bottle
FACILITIES gardens, par 3 golf course; sitting-room
CREDIT CARDS AE, MC, V **CHILDREN** possible **DISABLED** downstairs room **PETS** no dogs
CLOSED never **PROPRIETOR** Merv Griffin **MANAGER** Stephen Belton

CO MAYO/CO CLARE

CROSSMOLINA

ENNISCOE HOUSE

~ COUNTRY HOUSE HOTEL ~

Castlehill, near Crossmolina, Ballina, Co Mayo
TEL 096 31112 **FAX** 096 31773

SUSAN KELLETT'S FAMILY HOME, opened to guests since 1982, is a Georgian country house with a walled garden, set in wooded parkland on the shores of Lough Conn. The public rooms, with their open fires and family portraits, are lived-in and welcoming. There are canopy and four-poster beds in four of the period-style bedrooms. A one-bedroom house with an open fireplace in the sitting-room has been converted in traditional style for weekly stays. Susan Kellett produces fine, unfussy Irish country house food (including Irish cheeses). There are good trout and salmon fishing facilities.

~

NEARBY Moyne Abbey, 10 miles (16 km); Lough Conn.
LOCATION 12 miles (19 km) SW of Ballina, 2 miles (3 km) S of Crossmolina on Castlebar road; in parkland on 300-acre estate, with ample car parking
MEALS breakfast, dinner; wine licence
PRICES B&B I£44-I£76; DB&B I£66-I£86; reduced weekly, weekend and family rates
ROOMS 6; 3 double, 3 family rooms; all with bath; all rooms have central heating
FACILITIES sitting-room, dining-room; boating, fishing
CREDIT CARDS AE, MC, V
CHILDREN welcome
DISABLED not suitable **PETS** accepted only by special arrangement
CLOSED Oct to Mar **PROPRIETOR** Susan Kellett

KILLALOE

TINARANA HOUSE

~ COUNTRY GUEST-HOUSE ~

Killaloe, Co Clare
TEL 061 376966 **FAX** 061 375369 **E-MAIL** tinarana@tinet.ie

THIS AUSTERE, grey stone Victorian house overlooking Lough Derg has pitch pine floors, original shutters, windows and fireplaces, and a spectacular entrance hall and stairway. There are deer and horses in the grounds and plenty of woodland walks. It belongs to two local GPs who run a homeopathic clinic nearby and various courses are held at the house, such as 'Reinvigorate Yourself' or 'Immerse Yourself in Peace and Tranquillity'. It also welcomes guests who may have treatments in what used to be the old nursery, and use the basement steam room and sauna or the gym in what was the billiard room. Comfortable and quiet; huge airy rooms; chapel; good healthy breakfasts; helpful staff.

~

NEARBY walking; fishing; Killaloe; Limerick, 20 miles (32 km); Shannon.
LOCATION in gardens and grounds on edge of Lough Derg 4 miles (6 km) from Killaloe; ample parking
MEALS breakfast, lunch, dinner
PRICES rooms I£45-I£85pp; standard double I£130; breakfast included; lunch from I£10; dinner I£22.50 **ROOMS** 14; 8 double, 4 twin, 2 single; all with bath; all rooms with phone, tv; hairdrier on request
FACILITIES garden, terrace; sauna, steam room; gym; treatments **CREDIT CARDS** V
CHILDREN not suitable **DISABLED** not possible **PETS** not accepted **CLOSED** 24-27 Dec
PROPRIETORS Drs Pascal and Freida Carmody **MANAGER** Garrett Gavin

Co Galway

ROSLEAGUE MANOR

∼ COUNTRY HOUSE HOTEL ∼

Letterfrack, Connemara, Co Galway
TEL 095 41101 **FAX** 095 41168

WE VISITED RECENTLY and noted the polished decoration and service. It makes an interesting contrast to our other recommendations in the area (Crocnaraw, page 71): come here if you want a charming but more polished experience. Nigel Rush supervises the kitchen, which specializes in Connemara lamb and seafood (freshly delivered each evening), and makes much use of home-grown fruit and vegetables. Anne takes charge of the front of house, including the large, elegant dining-room fitted out in keeping with the Georgian building

∼

NEARBY Connemara National Park; Kylemore Abbey.
LOCATION one mile (1.6 km) W of Letterfrack, on shores of Ballinakill Bay; in 30-acre grounds; ample car parking
MEALS breakfast, light lunch, tea, dinner; full licence
PRICES B&B I£45-I£95; dinner from I£27; also à la carte
ROOMS 20 double (4 suites); all with bath; all rooms have central heating, phone
FACILITIES 3 sitting-rooms, bar, dining-room, conservatory, billiard room
CREDIT CARDS AE, MC, V **CHILDREN** accepted
DISABLED ramp to public rooms; access at rear to ground-floor bedroom
PETS dogs accepted in bedrooms by arrangement **CLOSED** Nov to Easter
PROPRIETORS Patrick and Anne Foyle

GARRAUNBAUN HOUSE

∼ COUNTRY GUEST-HOUSE ∼

Moyard, Co Galway
TEL/FAX 095 41649 **E-MAIL** finnegan@cybercable.tm.fr

ON OUR VISIT, we turned left at a group of donkeys gathered in the road, up a drive through an orchard and past the monkey puzzle tree to this pleasing early Victorian version of a Georgian manor house. It has starred in a number of continental fashion magazines. Even Delia Finnegan's cats have had their time in the sun as models. Everything here is charming and romantic; bedrooms are pink, green, lavender; bathrooms have French wallpaper and big bath towels; there's tartan in the library and a piano in the dining-room. Mrs Finnegan is an excellent cook and makes her own brown bread and yoghourt. Through an ironwork gate in the hedge is a path down to the seashore at Ballynakill Bay.

∼

NEARBY Innishboffin and Inishturk islands; Kylemore Abbey; fishing.
LOCATION in countryside between Letterfrack and Clifden; with parking
MEALS breakfast, dinner
PRICES rooms I£25-I£35pp; standard double I£70; breakfast included; dinner I£17
ROOMS 3; all double with bath; hairdrier available
FACILITIES garden, terrace
CREDIT CARDS MC, V **CHILDREN** not accepted **DISABLED** not possible
PETS not accepted **CLOSED** never
PROPRIETORS John and Catherine Finnegan

Co Mayo/Co Galway

Newport House

~ COUNTRY HOUSE HOTEL ~

Newport, Co Mayo
TEL 098 41222 FAX 098 41613 E-MAIL KJT1@anu.ie

FISHING IS THE PREOCCUPATION of most visitors to Newport House, which overlooks Newport river, though it is by no means the only attraction. The Georgian house is gracious and elegant, but the Thompsons encourage a caring, friendly attitude rather than super-slick professionalism in their staff. Bedrooms are spacious and individually decorated; a game-keeper's cottage is also available. Simplicity is the hallmark of the food, making full use of local Clew Bay seafood – and the kitchen does its own butchering as well as baking. Wines are Kieran's hobby.

~

NEARBY Blarney Castle, 12 miles (19 km); Joyce Country; golf
LOCATION on edge of town; ample car parking
MEALS breakfast, light lunch, dinner; full licence
PRICES B&B I£60-I£78; dinner I£32
ROOMS 18; 14 double, 2 single, 2 four-poster rooms; all with bath; some rooms in courtyard adjacent to main house; all rooms have phone
FACILITIES 2 sitting-rooms, bar, dining-room; fishing
CREDIT CARDS AE, DC, MC, V
CHILDREN accepted **DISABLED** access possible – ground-floor bedrooms
PETS accepted; not in main house or public rooms
CLOSED mid-Oct to mid-Mar; Christmas **PROPRIETORS** Kieran and Thelma Thompson

Currarevagh House

~ COUNTRY HOUSE HOTEL ~

Oughterard, Connemara, Co. Galway
TEL 091 552312 FAX 091 552731

THIS SOLID COUNTRY HOUSE on the leafy shores of Lough Corrib has been in the Hodgson family for five generations and its sense of traditional styles and standards meticulously preserved is quite overpowering. Many of the guests return for the fishing on the lough. Afternoon tea in the airy, spacious sitting-room is quite a ritual, as are the 'Edwardian' breakfasts. Rooms vary but all are spotless. Revisiting recently we were struck by its wonderful peaceful location, the charm of the Hodgsons and a certain eccentricity.

~

NEARBY Connemara; Joyce Country; Aran Islands; The Burren.
LOCATION 4 miles (6 km) NW of Oughterard; in 150-acre woodlands beside Lough Corrib, with ample car parking
MEALS breakfast, picnic-lunch, tea, dinner; licence
PRICES B&B I£45-I£65; dinner I£21; reductions for 3 nights or more
ROOMS 15; 12 double, 10 with bath, 2 with shower; 2 single, 1 with bath; 1 family room, with bath
FACILITIES 3 sitting-rooms (one with TV), bar, dining-room; tennis, boats, croquet, fishing
CREDIT CARDS not accepted **CHILDREN** accepted
DISABLED not ideal **PETS** accepted **CLOSED** Nov to Mar
PROPRIETORS Harry and June Hodgson

Co Kerry/Co Cork

ARDFERT

Barrow House

~ WATERSIDE GUEST-HOUSE ~

West Barrow, Ardfert, Co Kerry
TEL 066 7136437 **FAX** 066 7136402

THIS WHITE 18THC house and group of cottages on Barrow harbour is next to Arnold Palmer-designed Tralee golf course. As we went to press, it had just been sold, in the words of previous owner Maureen Erde, to "one of our local North Kerry millionaires who has hotels". Irish-American Mrs Erde has moved on to warmer climes in Portugal with her husband, Allan, closing the chapter of her life she wrote about in her wry and amusing memoir, *Help! I'm An Irish Innkeeper*. We don't know what happened to Seamus, the ghost who tinkers with electricity. Maybe he went to Portugal, too, but, if not, he can expect some major upgrading and upheavals to compete with his activities. Reports, please.

~

NEARBY golf at Tralee and Ballybunion; Ardfert; Tralee, 7miles (11 km).
LOCATION on Barrow harbour next to the Tralee golf club; with parking
MEALS breakfast
PRICES rooms I£37.50-I£40pp for suite for 2 people; standard double I£75; breakfast included
ROOMS 7 suites; 2 with 1 bedroom, 3 with 2 bedrooms, 2 with 3 bedrooms; 6 with bath, 1 with shower; hairdrier available **FACILITIES** terraces; harbour wall; restaurant; golf **CREDIT CARDS** MC, V **CHILDREN** by arrangement **DISABLED** not possible
PETS not possible **CLOSED** mid-Oct to 1 Apr **PROPRIETORS** Skellig Group

BALLYCOTTON

Spanish Point Seafood Restaurant

~ RESTAURANT WITH ROOMS ~

Ballycotton, Co Cork
TEL 021 646177 **FAX** 021 646179

WHAT ABOUT BAKED BLACK SOLE on the bone with a citrus butter, or marinated monkfish and prawn kebab on a bed of wild rice with two sauces for dinner? John Tattan brings fresh seafood home in his trawler to be cooked by his talented wife, Mary (trained by Darina Allen at Ballymaloe Cookery School), at their busy and renowned conservatory restaurant, Spanish Point, overlooking Ballycotton Bay in East Cork. It's a perfect end to the evening to go upstairs to one of these simple, unfussy rooms with pink carpets and showers. Two have sea views. For those with children, there is a baby-sitting service so that you won't be disturbed from your lobster, and a cot can be provided.

~

NEARBY Youghal; Midleton; Cloyne; walking; birdwatching; beaches.
LOCATION in clifftop position in fishing village; with parking
MEALS breakfast, lunch, dinner
PRICES rooms I£25pp; I£30 single; I£60 family room; breakfast included; lunch I£12; dinner I£21
ROOMS 5; 3 double, 2 family; all with shower; all rooms with phone, tv, tea/coffee making facilities
FACILITIES garden; tennis court; baby-sitting
CREDIT CARDS DC, MC, V **CHILDREN** welcome **DISABLED** not possible **PETS** accepted
CLOSED 2 Jan to 3 Feb **PROPRIETOR** Mary Tattan

Co Kerry/Co Cork

Cork

Arbutus Lodge

~ Town hotel ~

MiddleGlanmire Road, Montenotte, Cork, Co Cork
Tel 021 501237 **Fax** 021 502893 **E-mail** arbutus@iol.ie

ARBUTUS LODGE is a substantial suburban house, well known for its food and prize-winning terraced gardens planted with rare trees and shrubs, including the flowering shrub from which it takes its name. Sadly, owner Declan Ryan and his wife, Patsy, have sold the family restaurant and hotel – one of Cork's best-loved institutions – after 40 years. But the future of the celebrated cassoulet of prawns and ribs of beef in red wine sauce is secure: French chef Eric Theze has stayed on. New owner John Carmody is busy renovating and intends to enhance the original features of this former home of a Lord Mayor of Cork. Dine in the ballroom with gaslight fittings.

~

Nearby Blarney Castle, 6 miles (10 km).
Location ¼ mile (0.5 km) NE of middle of Cork; with garden and ample car parking
Meals breakfast, lunch, dinner; full licence
Prices B&B I£55-I£125; suites I£135-I£200; dinner I£26.50
Rooms 20; 12 double, all with bath, 4 also with shower; 8 single, 4 with bath, 4 with shower; all rooms have central heating, tv, phone, radio **Facilities** sitting-room, bar, dining-room **Credit cards** AE, DC, MC, V **Children** welcome if well-behaved
Disabled access difficult **Pets** not accepted **Closed** 23-28 Dec; restaurant only Sun (limited bar menu for residents) **Proprietor** John Carmody

Durrus

Blairs Cove House

~ Restaurant with rooms ~

Durrus, nr Bantry, Co Cork
Tel 027 61127 **Fax** 027 61487 **E-mail** blairscove@tinet.ie

THIS GEORGIAN HOUSE overlooking Dunmanus Bay is best known for its acclaimed restaurant in the converted stable block, which has an open wood-burning grill and enticing buffet – Sabine de Mey is passionate about her cooking. Around the rose-filled courtyard there are three sets of well-equipped rooms for B & B guests, in attractive, contemporary style, almost little homes in themselves. Blairs Cove 2 has a wall of glass, giving superb sea views, a bed in the upstairs 'loft' and a cosy wood-burning stove. Breakfast – fruit salad and yoghourt, four kinds of bread, ham, cheese, fruit, smoked salmon, freshly squeezed orange juice – is brought to your room. There are horses on the estate.

~

Nearby Bantry; Skibbereen; Schull.
Location in 4½ acres of gardens and grounds, 1½ miles (2 km) out of Durrus on Goleen/Barleycove road; ample parking
Meals breakfast, dinner (not Sunday or Monday)
Prices rooms I£50-I£65pp; standard double I£120; breakfast included; dinner I£30
Rooms 3; 1 double/twin with 2 bedrooms, 2 double; 2 with bath, 1 with shower; all with phone, tv, radio, video, hairdrier; kitchen; tea/coffee making facilities
Facilities garden, terraces; restaurant
Credit cards MC, V **Children** welcome **Disabled** not possible **Pets** no dogs
Closed never **Proprietors** Phillipe and Sabine de Mey

Co Fermoy/Co Cork

CASTLEHYDE

CASTLEHYDE HOTEL

~ COUNTRY HOTEL ~

Castlehyde, Fermoy, Co Cork
TEL 025 31865 **FAX** 025 31485 **E-MAIL** cashyde@iol.ie

WE HEARD SEVERAL REPORTS of the comfort and quiet of this new courtyard hotel in the converted Georgian dower house, stables and coach-houses of Castlehyde Castle, near Fermoy, in the Blackwater Valley. Owned and run by a Dutch couple, it is set in woodland beside the Blackwater River. Many of the original features have been retained, such as the stable clock, and there are some splendid pedimented gateways. The Mermaids Restaurant is open throughout the day. The library and sitting-room have antique furniture. Erik and Helen Speekenbrink decided they wanted to give guests as much opportunity as possible to sit outside, and the garden of their dower house is perfect in fine weather.

~

NEARBY Mallow, 18 miles (29 km); Fermoy, 2 miles (3 km); Cork.
LOCATION in countryside between Fermoy and Mallow; with parking
MEALS breakfast, lunch, dinner
PRICES rooms from I£85 to I£150; breakfast included; lunch from I£5; dinner from I£25.50 **ROOMS** 14; all double/twin; all with bath/shower; all rooms with phone, tv, hairdrier, tea/coffee making facilities; safe at reception
FACILITIES restaurant; garden; sitting-room, library **CREDIT CARDS** AE, DC, MC, V
CHILDREN accepted **DISABLED** possible **PETS** by arrangement **CLOSED** 10-31 Jan
PROPRIETORS Erik and Helen Speekenbrink

GLANDORE

THE MARINE HOTEL

~ HARBOURSIDE HOTEL ~

Glandore, Co Cork
TEL 028 33366 **FAX** 028 33600 **E-MAIL** cmv@indigo.ie

WHEN WE CALLED at this yellow family-run hotel on the little harbour at Glandore, some guests were sitting outside in the sun watching boats and Mr O'Brien was keeping an eye on the repainting of the annexe. It is a delightful and picturesque spot with plenty of character, but can, he warns, be very busy – and noisy – on Saturday nights, so annexe rooms are recommended for quiet. Four bedrooms overlook the sea. Rooms are smallish, functional, with gingham sheets and power showers. The Rectory restaurant is a short walk away and has sea views from its 19thC windows; more bedrooms are being planned here. The O'Briens have their own trawler, so seafood is fresh.

~

NEARBY Drombeg Stone Circle, 2 miles (3 km); Skibbereen; Union Hall.
LOCATION in village of Glandore, overlooking small harbour; parking available
MEALS breakfast, lunch, dinner
PRICES rooms I£38pp; standard double I£76; single I£35; breakfast included; lunch from I£5; dinner I£15
ROOMS 16; 8 double, 8 double with single bed; 14 with bath, 2 with shower; all with tv, hairdrier; tea/coffee making facilities
FACILITIES terrace overlooking harbour; bar; restaurant **CREDIT CARDS** AE, MC, V
CHILDREN welcome; free accommodation up to 14 **DISABLED** not suitable
PETS not accepted **CLOSED** 3 Nov to 15 Mar **PROPRIETOR** Sean O'Brien

Co Cork

GLANWORTH MILL

∼ COUNTRY GUEST-HOUSE ∼

Glanworth, Fermoy, Co Cork
TEL 025 38555 FAX 025 38560 E-MAIL glanworth@iol.ie

THIS NEWLY-RESTORED 1790s woollen mill – with working water wheel – on the banks of the River Funcheon in the lush, green Blackwater Valley is next to a Norman castle and an old bridge. It's a quiet place where you may see herons fishing and there are pretty walks along the river. Rooms are named after writers associated with the area, such as Anthony Trollope and novelist Elizabeth Bowen. The mill is eight miles (13 km) from her much-loved, now demolished, house, Bowen's Court; stones from the site were 'rescued' by owners Emelyn Heaps and his wife, Lynne Glasscoe, and have become part of the fireplace in the library. Breakfast in the tea-room or outside in the courtyard garden.

∼

NEARBY Fermoy, 5 miles (8 km); Trollope's house at Mallow; Kanturk.
LOCATION in riverside grounds and gardens in Blackwater Valley near Mallow; with parking MEALS breakfast, lunch, dinner PRICES rooms I£35-I£38pp; single supp I£10; standard double I£70; breakfast included; lunch from I£5; dinner I£20
ROOMS 11; all double/twin; all with bath/shower; all rooms with phone, hairdrier
FACILITIES courtyard garden; library, restaurant; tea room; trout fishing with fly
CREDIT CARDS DC, MC, V CHILDREN not possible DISABLED possible PETS not accepted
CLOSED 25-27 Dec PROPRIETORS Emelyn Heaps and Lynne Glasscoe

BLUE HAVEN HOTEL

∼ TOWN HOTEL ∼

3 Pearse Street, Kinsale, Co Cork
TEL 021 772209 FAX 021 774268 E-MAIL bluhaven@iol.ie

THIS BRIGHT YELLOW, blue-trimmed small hotel with an acclaimed seafood restaurant in the middle of Kinsale changed hands for a vast sum in the summer of 1999, and so change was in the air as we went to press. The Blue Haven has been much loved by the Irish and international media critics, and previous owners Brian and Anne Cronin's commitment and hard work was recognized by award after award for the successful pairing of excellent food and cosy, comfortable accommodation. In the words of Rabbi Blue, the Cronins managed to produce 'something very special, something personal and human'. We look forward to seeing what happens under new ownership and management and welcome reports.

∼

NEARBY Cork, 18 miles (29 km); golf at Old Head of Kinsale.
LOCATION in centre of town
MEALS breakfast, bar lunch, dinner
PRICES rooms I£75pp; standard double I£150; breakfast included; lunch from I£5; dinner I£27.50
ROOMS 17; all double (7 twin); most with bath, 4 with shower; all with phone, tv, hairdrier, iron, tea/coffee making facilities FACILITIES garden
CREDIT CARDS all major CHILDREN welcome DISABLED not possible upstairs
PETS not accepted CLOSED 24 and 25 Dec; 3-28 Jan
PROPRIETOR Bryan Greene MANAGERS Avril Greene and Marcus Mitchell

Co Cork/Co Kerry

Rivermount House

~ COUNTRY GUEST-HOUSE ~

Knocknabinny, Barrells Cross, Kinsale, Co Cork
TEL 021 778033 **FAX** 021 778225

CLAIRE O'SULLIVAN and her husband had this large, comfortable, traditional family house overlooking the Bandon River built for them eight years ago. Since then, nearby Kinsale Old Head golf course has established itself as one of the wilder golfing settings in Ireland. Surrounded by sea, you feel you are playing golf off the end of the world. Rivermount House, only a five-minute drive from the club house, offers a 10 per cent discount on green fees to guests. Generous breakfasts; large bedrooms with co-ordinated fabrics; beds with blankets; power showers. Mrs O'Sullivan, who used to be a hairdresser in Kinsale, is a welcoming hostess; bargain prices.

~

NEARBY Kinsale, 3 miles (5 km); Old Head golf course; Cork, 17 miles (27 km).
LOCATION in countryside, 2½ miles (4 km) S of Kinsale on the R600; in gardens with ample parking **MEALS** breakfast **PRICES** rooms I£22pp; standard double I£44; breakfast included **ROOMS** 6; 2 double, 1 twin, 3 family; all with power shower; all rooms with phone, tv, radio, hairdrier, tea/coffee making facilities; trouser press available **FACILITIES** sitting-room; garden **CREDIT CARDS** MC, V **CHILDREN** welcome; cot **DISABLED** no special facilities **PETS** not in house **CLOSED** 1 Dec to 1 Feb **PROPRIETOR** Claire O'Sullivan

Tahilla Cove Country House

~ WATERSIDE COUNTRY GUEST-HOUSE ~

Tahilla, near Sneem, Co Kerry
TEL 064 45204 **FAX** 064 45104 **E-MAIL** tahillacove@tinet.ie

THE TIDE RISES AND FALLS against the harbour wall of this private, little waterside retreat in exotic Gulf Stream gardens on the Ring of Kerry, where the Waterhouse family give you a warm welcome. The land was bought in 1947 by the late Charles Waterhouse (husband of Dolly and father of James), ADC to the Governor of the North West Frontier Province in India. He had found the 'most idyllic spot in Ireland or any other country' and so built a house here. Some rooms have balconies. The family are delightful hosts. Food is delicious. When we visited, dogs and children were happily rolling across the lawn by the harbour wall. Wonderful sunsets; walks through the woods along the coastline.

~

NEARBY Ring of Kerry; Killarney, 27 miles (43 km); lakes.
LOCATION in waterside gardens on N70 Ring of Kerry road, 11 miles (18 km) W of Kenmare and 5 miles (8 km) E of Sneem; ample parking **MEALS** breakfast, bar lunch, dinner **PRICES** rooms I£35- I£40pp (sea view); standard double I£80; breakfast included; lunch I£5; dinner I£18 **ROOMS** 9; 7 with double, 2 twin; 8 with bath, 1 with shower; all with phone, tv, radio, hairdrier; kettles on request. **FACILITIES** balconies; room service until 10pm; garden, terraces **CREDIT CARDS** AE, DC, MC, V **CHILDREN** welcome **DISABLED** possible **PETS** well-behaved dogs welcome by arrangement **CLOSED** mid-Oct to Easter **PROPRIETORS** the Waterhouse family

Co Cork

MARIA'S SCHOOLHOUSE

~ COUNTRY HOSTEL ~

Union Hall, Co Cork
TEL 028 33002 **FAX** 028 33002 **E-MAIL** mariasschoolhouse@tinet.ie

THIS VICTORIAN SCHOOLHOUSE has had its windows painted purple. On our visit, there were American backpackers in the dormitory up under the gabled roof. There is, indeed, an element of 'alternative' here – the idea of the place came from California. But it is happy, welcoming, and runs like clockwork. Professionalism and attention to detail underpin the whole approach. Maria and her staff like taking care of you and know how to do it. Delicious breakfasts include peaches and *crème fraîche*, French toast and savoury crepes. Bedrooms in pinks, mauves and greens have reading lights. Dine – on Thai perhaps – at a long table by the old classroom stove.

~

NEARBY Union Hall, 1 mile (1.5 km); Drombeg Stone Circle, 4 miles (6 km); Skibbereen.
LOCATION in countryside between village and Reen Pier; with parking
MEALS breakfast, dinner by prior arrangement **PRICES** rooms I£12-I£17pp; standard double I£24; dormitory I£8pp; breakfast I£3.50 -I£5; dinner I£15 **ROOMS** 8 and a dormitory; 6 double, 2 family; all with shower; bathroom available; hairdrier on request **FACILITIES** garden; baby-sitting; badminton, kayaking, bicycles; self-catering kitchen **CREDIT CARDS** MC, V **CHILDREN** welcome **DISABLED** wheelchair friendly; 1 wheelchair room and bathroom **PETS** not in house **CLOSED** end Oct to mid-Mar
PROPRIETORS Maria Hoare and Jim Kennedy

CO WATERFORD/CO WICKLOW

RICHMOND HOUSE

∽ COUNTRY HOUSE AND RESTAURANT ∽

Cappoquin, Co Waterford
TEL 058 54278 FAX 058 54988 E-MAIL richmond@amireland. com

ALMOST THE FIRST THING you notice when you walk into the hall is the black cast iron wood-burning stove that has been there, so it is said, since the house was built in 1704 for the Earl of Cork and Burlington. This is a traditional, friendly, family-run guest-house, with a good, well-frequented restaurant; Paul Deevy, son of the house, is an accomplished chef and his dishes can be classic and traditional, or with a dash of foreign influence, using fresh herbs and local produce. His wife, Claire, plays jazz over the sound system as she serves dinner on white tablecloths. Bedrooms are traditional, too, with dark antique furniture, some mahogany bedsteads, and vases of fresh flowers. Tea is served in the conservatory.

∽

NEARBY Dungarvan, 10 miles (16 km); Waterford, 40 miles (64 km); Cork, 45 miles (72 km).
LOCATION in gardens and grounds just outside village; with parking
MEALS breakfast, lunch **PRICES** rooms I£40-I£60pp; standard double I£100; breakfast included; dinner I£29 **ROOMS** 9; 2 double, 3 twin, 3 double and single, 1 single; 8 with bath, 1 with shower only; all with phone, tv, hairdrier; some with trouser press; all with tea/coffee making facilities **FACILITIES** conservatory; garden, terraces **CREDIT CARDS** AE, DC, MC, V **CHILDREN** welcome **DISABLED** no facilities **PETS** not accepted **CLOSED** 20 Dec to 10 Feb **PROPRIETORS** the Deevy family

RATHSALLAGH HOUSE

∽ COUNTRY HOUSE AND RESTAURANT ∽

Dunlavin, Co Wicklow
TEL 045 403112 FAX 045 403343 E-MAIL info@rathsallagh.com

THE O'FLYNNS SAY THAT these converted Queen Anne stables are much more than just a business: it is their home and their life. They have managed something remarkable in creating one of the best-equipped and most comfortable and respected country house hotels in Ireland, while at the same time giving as much thought to the importance of a warm welcome, informality and hospitality. You can pick raspberries in the kitchen garden and have your Victorian country house breakfast served to you from the sideboard by a butler. Classic food, with many home-grown ingredients. Some ground-floor bedrooms. Located an hour's drive from Dublin in the heart of racing country.

∽

NEARBY Glendalough; Russborough; Powerscourt; National Stud.
LOCATION in gardens and 530-acre grounds, 2½ miles (4 km) S of Dunlavin; with parking
MEALS breakfast, lunch, dinner
PRICES rooms I£55 to I£95pp; standard double I£150; breakfast included; lunch from I£7; dinner I£30 **ROOMS** 17; 11 double, 6 twin; all with bath; all with phone, tv, hairdrier, tea/coffee making facilities **FACILITIES** pool; sauna; massage; 18-hole golf course; tennis court; snooker; riding and hunting by arrangement
CREDIT CARDS AE, DC, MC, V **CHILDREN** under 12 not accepted **DISABLED** wheelchair friendly **PETS** by arrangement **CLOSED** Christmas **PROPRIETORS** Joe and Kay O'Flynn

Co Kilkenny/Co Wexford

KILKENNY

HILLGROVE

∽ COUNTRY BED-AND-BREAKFAST ∽

Warrington, Bennettsbridge Road, Kilkenny, Co Kilkenny
TEL 056 51453/22890 FAX 056 51453

MARGARET DRENNAN used to work for the Irish Tourist Board before she opened up her neat, friendly family home to guests and she's a winner of a National Breakfast award. You start the day well, with, among other dishes, American-style pancakes with maple syrup, topped with natural yoghourt, chopped banana and honey. Hillgrove is an immaculate white house, covered with creeper, a quiet, comfortable place to stay on the road into busy Kilkenny (Margaret has a useful map of the town that she gives out to guests), and hard to beat on price. Often there's quite a crowd gathered in the sitting-room, chatting over a cup of tea. Bedrooms uncluttered, with good beds and some antiques.

∽

NEARBY Kilkenny, 2 miles (3 km); Thomastown, 8 miles (13 km).
LOCATION 2 miles (3 km) SE of Killkenny on the R700 Bennettsbridge to New Ross road; with parking
MEALS breakfast **PRICES** rooms I£18pp; standard double I£36; breakfast included
ROOMS 5; 2 double, 2 twin, 1 double and single; 1 with bath, 4 with shower; all rooms with hairdrier, electric blanket
FACILITIES sitting-room; garden **CREDIT CARDS** all major **CHILDREN** welcome
DISABLED not possible **PETS** not accepted **CLOSED** Dec and Jan
PROPRIETORS Margaret and Tony Drennan

TAGOAT

CHURCHTOWN HOUSE

∽ COUNTRY GUEST-HOUSE ∽

Tagoat, Rosslare, Co Wexford
TEL/FAX 053 32555

THIS WHITE, Georgian converted farmhouse sits serenely in its flat, green, somewhat windswept surroundings a few miles from Rosslare ferry port. On our visit, the grounds were filled with bluebells. There have been many additions around the rear courtyard and other old farm buildings, but Patricia Cody hates 'hotelification' and has tried to keep things to a personal, homely scale. She won't have kettles or hospitality trays in bedrooms, preferring, instead, to give individual service. She serves sherry before dinner so that she can introduce guests to each other. Care and thought has gone into everything here, from the walking sticks in the hall to the decoration and high standard of comfort.

∽

NEARBY Rosslare ferry port, 3 miles (5 km); Wexford; bird-watching on marshes.
LOCATION in gardens and grounds, half a mile (0.8 km) off N25 between Wexford and Rosslare harbour; 3 miles (5 km) from ferry port
MEALS breakfast, dinner **PRICES** rooms I£30-I£40pp; standard double I£60; breakfast included; dinner I£19.50 **ROOMS** 12; 6 double, 5 twin, 1 single; 9 with bath, 3 with shower; all rooms with phone, tv, electric blanket; hairdrier available **FACILITIES** gardens, terrace; croquet **CREDIT CARDS** AE, MC, V **CHILDREN** over 10 accepted; otherwise by arrangement **DISABLED** 1 wheelchair-friendly room **PETS** not accepted **CLOSED** 3 Nov to 1 Mar **PROPRIETORS** Patricia and Austin Cody

Co Dublin

The Fitzwilliam

∽ Town guest-house ∽

41 Upper Fitzwilliam Street, Dublin 2
Tel 01 662 5155/5044 **Fax** 01 676 7488

THIS UNPRETENTIOUS AND RELIABLE guest-house in an attractive street in the heart of Georgian Dublin is what used to be The Fitzwilliam before anyone ever even dreamed of opening the modern, new, minimalist Conran-designed Fitzwilliam Hotel on St Stephen's Green. Very reasonable and competitive special events rates make this a popular place to stay for rugby internationals. Irish breakfasts served in the charming small restaurant downstairs. Bedrooms, in Georgian colours, are elegant, unfussy, comfortable and spacious. Bathrooms are spotless. Friendly staff and private parking facilities give added value for those who like to stay in small, intimate quarters in the middle of the city.

∽

Nearby St Stephen's Green; Merrion Square; Trinity College.
Location in heart of Georgian Dublin, a short walk from St Stephen's Green; with parking
Meals breakfast, lunch, dinner **Prices** rooms I£30 to I£41pp; standard double I£80; breakfast included; lunch I£7; dinner I£20 **Rooms** 12; 5 double, 5 twin, 2 single; 2 with bath, 10 with shower; all rooms with phone, tv, hairdrier; tea/coffee making facilities **Facilities** sitting-room, restaurant **Credit cards** all major
Children welcome **Disabled** not possible **Pets** accepted **Closed** 21-31 Dec
Manager Declan Carney

The Grey Door

∽ Restaurant with rooms ∽

22-23 Upper Pembroke Street, Dublin 2
Tel 01 676 3286 **Fax** 01 676 3287

THIS TALL GEORGIAN HOUSE in the centre of Dublin has a discreet entrance and two restaurants, The Grey Door and Pier 32. When we called, it had been sold and was about to be refurbished, so changes may be expected. However, although carpets were somewhat worn, the rooms we saw were comfortable and furnished in traditional style, with good fabrics and some antique furniture. The attractive bathrooms have white tiles, brass fittings and heated towel rails. Downstairs, the restaurant offers 'modern Irish' cuisine. In the basement, the popular Pier 32 has rough flagstone floors, open fires, and is decorated with lobster pots and fishing nets. There is live music every night and it stays open until late. Reports welcome.

∽

Nearby Temple Bar; Grafton Street; Trinity College; shops.
Location 5 minutes walk from St Stephen's green; no parking available
Meals breakfast, lunch (weekdays), dinner
Prices rooms I£80-I£115; standard double I£80; (with breakfast included on weekends only); breakfast I£5 or I£6.95; lunch I£20 max; dinner I£35
Rooms 7; 3 double/twin, 4 family; all with bath; all rooms with phone, tv, radio, hairdrier, trouser press; safe in reception
Facilities sitting-room, 2 restaurants **Credit cards** all major **Children** accepted
Disabled not suitable **Pets** not accepted **Closed** Christmas Day, 1 day at Easter
Manager Simon Povall

Co Offaly/Co Meath

Birr

TULLANISK

~ Country house ~

Birr, Co Offaly
Tel 0509 20572 **Fax** 0509 21783 **E-mail** tnisk@indigo.ie

GEORGE GOSSIP is chairman of The Hidden Ireland, the group of private country house owners who welcome guests to their special homes. He is also a renowned and engaging 'hands on' host, and visitors to this 18thC dower house belonging to nearby Gothic Revival Birr Castle may be assured of amusement and entertainment. The house has been carefully restored by George and his wife, Susie, who are both excellent cooks – game is a speciality. This is classic Irish country house territory: candlelit dinners on family china around the table in the Georgian dining-room, plenty of games to play and books to read in front of the fire for rainy afternoons. Deer graze in the surrounding parkland.

~

Nearby Birr (heritage town); Birr Castle gardens.
Location in deer park and 700 acres of woodland, 1 mile (1.5 km) NW of Birr on R439 to Banagher **Meals** breakfast, packed lunch by request, dinner
Prices rooms I£38-I£50pp; standard double I£100; dinner I£25 **Rooms** 7; 3 double, 2 twin, all with bath; 1 twin and 1 double sharing shower room; phone, hairdrier on request **Facilities** deckchairs on lawn; woodland walks; board games
Credit cards MC, V **Children** welcome **Disabled** no special facilities **Pets** accepted if well-trained **Closed** Christmas **Proprietors** George and Susie Gossip

Oldcastle

LOUGHCREW HOUSE

~ Country guest-house ~

Oldcastle, Co Meath
Tel 049 8541356 **Fax** 049 8541722 **E-mail** cnaper@tinet.ie

THE NAPER FAMILY has lived here for 400 years, but all that remains (after several fires) of the 19thC neoclassical Loughcrew House (designed by the English architect Charles Cockerell) is a heap of stones and the reconstructed columns of the portico. Charles Naper and his wife, Emily, who runs a school of gilding and decorative finishes in the stable yard, welcome guests to the restored conservatory where they live. This is a beautiful, peaceful, friendly place, with moonlit ruins, log fires, long walks across the estate, romantic rooms with gilding and decorating by Emily, and delicious food cooked by Charles with produce from his kitchen garden. Country life with a difference.

~

Nearby Loughcrew Cairns; Dunsany Castle; Birr Castle Demesne.
Location in gardens and parkland, 3 miles (5 km) from Oldcastle; with parking
Meals breakfast, lunch
Prices rooms I£35pp; standard double I£70; single supp I£10; breakfast included; dinner I£20
Rooms 3; 1 double; 2 twin; 1 with bath, 2 with shower; hairdrier on request
Facilities gardens; private sitting-room; tennis court, bicycles, walking, lakes
Credit cards all major **Children** welcome **Disabled** downstairs rooms **Pets** not accepted **Closed** Christmas Day **Proprietors** Charles and Emily Naper

Co Westmeath/Co Kildare

Mearescourt House

∽ Country house ∽

Rathconrath, Mullingar, Co Westmeath
Tel/Fax 044 55112

T HIS GEORGIAN HOUSE of grand proportions is in a beautiful setting, with few other buildings to be seen for miles around. On our visit, sheep were attractively arranged in the green parkland dotted with chestnut trees. It's serene, quiet, very 18thC; no wonder some Dublin politicians use it as a bolt-hole from their rather different world. Eithne Pendred – she and her husband, Brendan, used to have a small hotel in Cavan – is an excellent cook and regularly sends herself off on courses. She makes her own marmalade and ice cream. Potatoes, vegetables, soft fruit and herbs come from the walled garden. Rooms are large, comfortable and restful. Guests eat at small tables for dinner. Lovely walks.

∽

Nearby Mullingar, 9 miles (14 km); Dublin, 49 miles (79 km); Castlepollard; Tullynally.**Location** in gardens and parkland, 1 mile (1.6 km) from Rathconrath village; with parking **Meals** breakfast, lunch **Prices** rooms I£27.50pp; standard double I£55; breakfast included; dinner I£18.50 **Rooms** 4; 2 double, 1 twin, 1 double and single; all with bath and shower; tv and hairdrier available on request **Facilities** gardens, terrace; lakeside and woodland walks **Credit cards** AE, MC, V **Children** welcome **Disabled** no special facilities **Pets** not in house, but can sleep in car **Closed** Christmas week **Proprietors** Eithne and Brendan Pendred

Barberstown Castle

∽ Castle and country house ∽

Straffan, Co Kildare
Tel 01 6288157 **Fax** 01 6277027 **E-mail** castleir@iol.ie

T HERE'S MUCH HISTORY in the walls of this cluster of buildings that includes a 13thC castle, a classic Georgian country house, and a medieval house, one of the few in Ireland to have been occupied for more than 400 years. A new wing of bedrooms has recently been added. The owners' list is as fascinating: John Blackwell erected the scaffold on which Charles I was executed; Hugh Barton, of the wine family, moved from here in the 19thC when he built what is now the Kildare Hotel and Country Club; rock star Eric Clapton. Bedrooms are elegant and comfortable, some with four-posters. The restaurant (half Georgian, half medieval) and the hotel has won awards for its hospitality, care and courtesy.

∽

Nearby Maynooth, 4 miles (6 km); Naas; Russborough House; Punchestown. **Location** in gardens and grounds between Maynooth and Straffan; with parking **Meals** breakfast, bar lunch, dinner **Prices** rooms I£66-I£77pp; standard double I£132; single supp I£10; suites I£154 per room; breakfast included; dinner I£31 **Rooms** 21; all double/twin; all with bath and shower; all rooms with phone, tv, radio, hairdrier, trouser press **Facilities** gardens; riding, fishing, shooting, golf, tennis **Credit cards** AE, DC, MC, V **Children** not under 12 **Disabled** possible **Pets** not accepted **Closed** 3 days at Christmas **Proprietor** Kenneth C Healy

HOTEL NAMES

H O T E L   N A M E S

Hotel Names

HOTEL NAMES

Hotel Locations

Hotel Locations

HOTEL LOCATIONS

HOTEL LOCATIONS